J. Panton

FREEDOM
A Call to Healing

Freedom a Call to Healing

Published by Kingdom Publishing, LLC
1350 Blair Drive Suite F
Odenton, Maryland 21113

Printed in the United States of America

Copyright © 2023 by J Panton

All rights reserved. No part of this book may be reproduced or transmitted in any form or by any means, electronic or mechanical, including photocopying, recording or by any information storage and retrieval system without written permission from the author, except for the inclusion of brief quotations in a review.

Ordering Information:
Quantity sales. Special discounts are available on quantity purchases by corporations, associations, and others. For details, contact the publisher at the address above.

ISBN 978-1-947741-93-5 *paperback*
ISBN 978-1-947741-94-2 *eBook*

Contents

Introduction		1
Chapter 1	My Journey to Eternal Freedom & Healing	7
Chapter 2	My Invitation into the Struggle	13
Chapter 3	Unresolved Scars from Our Past will Affect Our Future	17
Chapter 4	The Failing Education System	23
Chapter 5	Bring Back the Good Old Days	29
Chapter 6	Our Mental Fortitude	37
Chapter 7	The Freedom We Seek	41
Chapter 8	The Deception of the American Dream	47
Chapter 9	The Absolute Power of Law Enforcement	51
Chapter 10	The Great Divide	57
Chapter 11	The Rise of Fascism in Western Civilization	65
Chapter 12	The Tug of War	71
Chapter 13	The Battle for Our Beliefs	81
Chapter 14	We are Overcomers	87
Chapter 15	Arise	93
Chapter 16	A Call to Deal with the Past	97
Chapter 17	A Call to Healing	101

Chapter 18	A Call to Forgiveness	105
Chapter 19	The Gift of Forgiveness	109
Chapter 20	Stages of Deliverance	113
Chapter 21	The Call to Serve and Connect to Jesus	117
Chapter 22	Invitation to Thirst	123
Chapter 23	A Call to Prayer	127
Chapter 24	A Prayer of Comfort	133
Conclusion		135
Table of Reference		137
About the Author		139

Introduction

The ideals of freedom and justice for all are innovative notions that can be found at the heart of America. These ideals are embodied in the Declaration of Independence and protected by the Constitution. However, freedom and justice for all, especially for African Americans, has been elusive. African Americans have fought to obtain it through social movements and struggle at the risk of lives, blood, sweat, and tears.

The civil rights movement addressed the laws, customs, and practices that oppressed African American people. Moreover, our need for emotional, spiritual, and physiological healing has never been addressed. Though we have more physical freedoms than we have ever enjoyed, to maximize the freedoms and opportunities we have in the United States of America, we must be healed from centuries of scars and destructive programming.

If we don't seek the eternal freedom and healing we need as a people, it's like building a house on a cracked foundation. We are bound at some point to collapse, and we are never truly free to tap into our full potential as human beings. The Bible says it this way: You cannot pour new wine into old wine skins, and by the grace of God, we have made it this far.

We must face the fact that in the same manner, racism did not magically disappear from society after the Civil Rights but was passed down from generation to generation and built into the institutions. Likewise, centuries of destructive, institutionalized, and dehumanizing psychological programming were passed down from generation to generation. These unspoken truths are wreaking havoc in our communities. I believe there is a call for us to seek the healing and deliverance that we need to have lasting peace and prosperity in our communities.

It is time for us, as African Americans living in the United States, to redefine for ourselves what it truly means to be black in America. In many ways, we have been fulfilling the negative stereotypes that we were psychologically and systematically programmed to believe in ourselves. Moreover, we have defeated the myths about our intellectual inabilities and limitations. We have proven to society that we are a force to reckon with when we believe and embrace our God-given worth, abilities, and potential.

However, far too many are still struggling to overcome systematic programming and have accepted the lies that we are not able to overcome and self-govern. Far too many have accepted less and see failure as the norm. Far too many are self-destructive, and the only solutions offered by society are usually law and order and the prison system. We must take a step back and look at what is true about who we are as a people and begin to write a new chapter to undo the psychological systematic programming that is still hindering us. We are a resilient and forgiving people. It is time for us to overcome—not just outwardly, but to overcome from within.

In 2012, the Lord impressed upon me the need to pray for the African American community. I felt the need to pray against the spirit of oppression that was being felt by the people. The shedding of innocent blood in the streets, the issue of mental illness, the increased numbers of those incarcerated, and the injustices in the school system of the United States of America sent me to my knees.

Likewise, to pray against the false hope we place in politicians to correct the issues we face and to follow through on their promises once elected. To pass common-sense legislation to increase our equity and quality of life, but time and time again, through their inaction, we are forced to wait and hope for a change that is far too often deferred. The road to freedom and equality is bumpy, and it requires patience, determination, and perseverance.

It is very difficult to change the mind and consciousness of a person so that they empathize with your pain—a pain they have never experienced. It is also difficult to have them acknowledge the

Introduction

scars they have caused, especially if it puts them in an unfavorable light and exposes the darkness in their hearts.

It is far easier for them to convince themselves that they have done nothing wrong and the "privilege" they are enjoying is because of hard work rather than a system that was set up to purposefully advance their interest by systematically oppressing others.

Moreover, it is even more difficult to admit the wrongdoing of the Forefathers of America. If doing so, it leads to the "leveling of the playing field," which would result in real "justice for all." It is a fact that some believe slavery was a "necessary evil" to build the U.S. economy and its industries. In turn, this mindset eliminates empathy and the attitude that more needs to be done to address the inequities in the United States. It further desensitizes their minds from understanding that the system of slavery has had a detrimental, long-lasting, and sustained effect on not just those who directly experienced it but on multiplied generations thereafter.

When discontentment is expressed about how African Americans are treated and the lack of equity in our strive for life, liberty, and the pursuit of happiness. We are seen as lazy complainers who are essentially stuck in a perpetual victim mentality. The thoughts against us are hostile and indifferent. Statements such as, "Just pick yourself up by your bootstraps"—meaning, do something without any outside help—further desensitizes others from truly understanding the frailty of human nature and its tendency to break under extreme pressures. It is far easier to say "they" should be satisfied with the opportunities they have now and the gains they have made and simply move on.

In the history of America, other human beings seem to get the empathy to mourn, acknowledge, and build memorials after a trauma occurs in their lives. All except the black race. We have experienced sustained trauma mentally, physically, emotionally, and spiritually in the Western Hemisphere that lasted well over four hundred years. Even after slavery, systems such as Jim Crow, segregation, and the systematic racism of today, our people were expected to just pick up the pieces of life, adjust, and live as law-abiding citizens. We were expected to live in self-denial with multiple generations worth of pain and physiological programming, as if the scars we are carrying are healed or just don't exist.

Our trauma was to remain inside and eat away at us just like a cancer. It is too painful for us to release it and risk damaging the image of our oppressors. Therefore, the memories of pain and abuse passed down by our ancestors still reside inside us at the level of our DNA. The pain is essentially destroying us from the inside out and the people around us. We are carriers of pain caused by centuries of oppression. Still, there has been no real remedy to cure us of these ills.

The statistics are heartbreaking. Forty-one percent of black males will not graduate from high school. One in three black males can expect to spend time in prison. One in one hundred black women are in prison. Seventy-one percent of black children are born to unmarried mothers. Only thirty percent of African Americans are married. These are tragedies that have not occurred by chance. These statistics are a result of the intentional destruction of the black male and female, which successfully resulted in the destruction of the black family unit—the foundation of a healthy nation of people.

Thus, the most important component we need as a community is hope. This is the hope of redemption offered by a loving and merciful God. He is not a God who only visits us for a few hours on Sunday mornings, nor a God to be called upon only in times of distress. He is a God who eagerly awaits a personal and constant relationship with each of us. The Bible is clear that Jesus Christ is tender-hearted towards the oppressed, despised, broken-hearted, those who are hopeless, and outcast and His heart toward us is unchangeable. He alone truly understands the pain we have endured, as the Bible says in Hebrew 4:15 KJV: *"For we have not, a High Priest which cannot be touched with the feelings of our infirmities; but was in all points tempted as we are, yet without sin"*. Jesus alone can restore us and heal us where we hurt. He alone can take our pain and turn it into purpose.

Introduction

On the night of March 1, 2014, I had an encounter with the Lord. That night, for the first time, I understood how the prophet Isaiah felt when the Lord called and said: *"I will go, send me"* (Isaiah 6:8). I, too, said to the Lord, send me. Even if I do not know or understand it all, I will submit myself to your will. It was at that moment that the Lord gave me the inspiration and revelation to write this book for African Americans who feel forgotten and left out of God's plan for humanity. This is a call to the African American community to come back to our loving Father for the healing we so desperately need. This is the only way for us to become our best selves in Him.

As you read this book, I pray you will come to understand that for us to receive the total freedoms we seek, we must first deal with the battleground in our minds. To have victory and become all God has called us to be, we must first understand how to break the bondage of our thoughts and minds. We do this by knowing our true worth and purpose for which we were created. Our worth is not determined by our situation, it is not given through material possessions, and it is not determined by people, but our worth comes from God. The one who created us with His purpose in mind.

"I, the LORD, have called you in righteousness; I will take hold of your hand. I will keep you and will make you to be a covenant for the people and a light for the Gentiles, to open eyes that are blind, to free captives from prison and to release from the dungeon those who sit in darkness. I am the LORD; that is my name! I will not yield my glory to another or my praise to idols. See, the former things have taken place, and new things I declare; before they spring into being I announce them to you." (Isaiah 42:6-9)

Freedom a Call to Healing

Chapter 1
My journey to Eternal Freedom & Healing

On January 9th, 1980, I was born in Portland, Jamaica. When I was approximately three years old, my mother emigrated to the United States in search of a better life for my sister and me. She was a single mother of two children with limited economic opportunities. It was her dream to give my sister and me a future where we had a choice and were not forced to make poor decisions due to our limited opportunities.

From the age of three onward, I was raised by my aunt and my grandparents. As a child, you don't have the capability to understand why decisions are made and why things are the way they are; you can only identify with how you feel in the moment. As a child, I felt abandoned by my parents, and as much as I was loved by my grandparents, the love I was shown could not replace my feelings of abandonment.

Throughout the diaspora, it is customary for children to be raised by grandparents. I remember as a child that there were six grandchildren, including myself, who were raised by my grandparents. All throughout the diaspora, you have parents who lack natural affection for their children, and you have a generation of children who are raining themselves or being raised by technology. I believe this unnatural affection is an effect of centuries of slavery.

You have children having children, except there are no grandparents to impart wisdom and guidance. Today's grandparents lack life experience, because they themselves are sometimes in their twenties and thirties and are still trying to figure out life. Throughout the diaspora, grandparents are the foundation of the black family. I can't image where I would be without my grandparents and how they sacrificed their happiness and comfort for the next generation;

I don't know where I would be today without my grandparents' wisdom and guidance.

As grandparents and great-grandparents in our communities are passing on, one could argue that there is a direct correlation with the lawlessness among young black men in their teens. Coupled with the fact that almost fifty percent of young black men graduate high school. There is a leadership vacuum in our communities that is being filled by the streets.

We have a generation of young men and women who lack purpose and love. Grandparents helped stabilize our communities and often pointed us to a relationship with God. Beyond just filling the void that our parents' absence leaves, they help us develop a "God conscience," which is lacking in today's young people. Though grandparents cannot fill the wounds caused by our parents' absence, their impact on our lives is indelible. They offer us unconditional love, safety, and stability.

I remember growing up asking myself what was wrong with me because I felt mentally and emotionally disconnected. It was very difficult for me to connect with my surroundings and those in my life who truly loved me at the time. I had a lot of anger and frustration because I missed having my parents.

Looking back now, I was most likely depressed. My ability to focus on school was affected, and by the age of six, I mentally gave up on learning. The next three years of my academic journey were impacted, and I showed absolutely zero effort in school. I remember turning ten years old, I did not know the letters of the alphabet, and I could not even spell my own name.

I was floating from grade to grade, not learning anything, and I was physically present but mentally checked out. However, my grandparents imparted the importance of an education because they themselves did not graduate high school. In those days, men in my family were academically illiterate because they had to forego school to help on the farm. I was raised in an agricultural community.

Even though I was prone to give in to peer pressure, the God conscience I developed having to attend church every Sunday always pulled me back when I lost my way. Attending Elementary School, for me at the time, was a way to get out of my community and experience something different. I was heading towards fulfilling the generational curse of becoming another male in my family who was illiterate.

It wasn't until my fifth-grade teacher looked beyond my limitations and saw me as a person that I believed this was a divine intervention. I believe this was a divine intervention because I was walking by her one day, as I have done many times before. This time, she stopped me and said, "There is something special about you, and I want to help you."

Those words unleashed something in me because no one up to that point in my life had ever seen that I had potential. I was always seen as the one who got in trouble and struggled academically. She began to work with me after school by giving me basic spelling words to practice and assigning me extra homework. For the first time in my life, I became focused on learning to read, and by the age of eleven, I could read.

The best gift I was given by my grandparents was that every Sunday, I had to go to church. At the age of fourteen, I heard the voice of the Lord telling me to serve Him. The Lord spoke into my heart and told me His purpose for me was to restore broken lives. Based on God's word to me, from that day on, my life changed in a significant way. Even though I did not surrender my life to the Lord at the of fourteen, the words I heard from the Lord gave me a sense of purpose. The spoken word from the Lord changed my life. By the end of my senior year in middle school, I went from the bottom of my class to graduating as the school's valedictorian and the most improved student.

"Then said Jesus to those Jews which believed on him, if ye continue in my word, then are ye my disciples; indeed, and ye shall know the truth, and the truth shall make you free" (John 8:31-32).

I met my mother in person for the first time when I emigrated to the United States at age seventeen. She spent over fourteen years fighting to gain her own legal status and was later able to secure legal status for my sister and me with the help of my stepfather. Even though my mother and I spent over fourteen years apart, there were many unresolved issues. The Lord began using her to play a vital role in my healing process. She consistently gave me sermons to listen to that talked about forgiveness and healing. I distinctly remember one sermon series from Dr. Charles Stanley on how the "Truth Can Set You Free." The truth about how God sees me—the individual—is not based on my circumstances.

As I continued to listen to the sermons and read the bible, the Lord started to give me revelation and insight as I listened to the messages. Therefore, I developed a burning desire to seek God more and build a relationship with him. I rediscovered that He had a "real" plan and purpose for my life. The brokenness I had suffered was all a part of His divine plan. The word of God began to repair me from all the years of low self-esteem, hurt, unforgiveness, anger, and feelings of abandonment. As I learned who He was through the help of the holy spirit, I could see who I was in Him.

It does not matter how our stories began and the life we were dealt—in Christ Jesus, there is hope. I have seen so many people who society has given up on and I see the difference it makes when they get to know who they are in Christ. It does not matter how you are labeled or treated by society; to rise above your situation, you must know who you are. When you understand and embrace your worth, you discover that there is more to life than what you see and experience.

Should I have accepted the fact I was raised without my parents at an age and that my child should be subjected to the same outcome? No, as I have come to know myself in Christ Jesus, I look at my family lineage and made the decision that I did not want to repeat the generational struggles of my father, who was also not raised by his own parents.

I can remember at the age of fifteen, I looked at my life and thought I wanted better for my future. I looked at my life and saw that if God did not intervene when I had children, it would be a repeat of the generational cycle, children who were not raised by their parents. I did not want my children to be fatherless because I was fatherless. I did not want my children to be broken because I was broken.

Even though I did not know how to be or become what I desired, I just knew that I wanted more. One night I began to picture my future and said, Lord, I want better for my life and my future children. At that moment, I fell to my knees and said, Father, in the name of Jesus, it is my heart's desire that I will not have children out of marriage. I prayed that my children would be born into a household with both mother and father fully present. I prayed that my children would feel wanted and loved. Help me to become my best self.

The prayer in that moment came from a place of pain and feeling abandoned. I had a deep desire in my heart to not repeat the mistakes of my parents. I felt it was my purpose to break generational curses and chart a new course for my destiny. I believe God honored that prayer, and that prayer shaped the course for what's to come in my future.

It is such an awesome thing when I can look back on my life and see Jesus in my struggles. At that moment, I felt comforted and evolved from a place of victimhood to feeling empowered and victorious. Before seeing the Lord in the pain of my childhood, it felt like life happened to me, and I felt victimized. When I saw the Lord in my struggles, he allowed me to see the full picture and to see his hands at work: Protecting me, covering me, loving me, and being a father to me.

It took away my bitterness and unforgiveness. It allowed me to embrace my story and it is healing to know that all along, God had a plan for my life. It is freeing to receive the truth that my life is worth more to God than any material possession. It also allows me to see things from the perspective of the person who caused me hurt and gives me the ability to empathize with them. It sets me free to approach the person with compassion instead of accusation. It sets you free from the strongholds of the past and allows me to see the benefits of my pain. It was with that new perspective that I was able to forgive my parents.

Today, I have been married for over fifteen years and am the proud father of two children who were born in our marriage. The Lord has blessed me to see my mother's and grandparents' prayers for my life realized.

Romans 5:3-5: "Not only so, but we also glory in our sufferings, because we know that suffering produces perseverance; perseverance, character; and character, hope. And hope does not put us to shame because God's love has been poured out into our hearts through the Holy Spirit, who has been given to us."

Chapter 2
My Invitation into the Struggle

Upon graduating from Harry S Truman High School in Bronx, New York at the age of Nineteen, I went to Buffalo State College to pursue a degree in Criminal Justice. My goal after graduating college was to become a police officer. I was passionate about serving and giving back to where I live. I thought becoming an officer would allow me to protect and serve my community. Growing up in Jamaica, I had family members and friends who were police officers. I always admired their work and how much they were loved and respected by the members of my community.

Living in the Bronx, New York, during the Mayor Giuliani era, my perception of law enforcement began to change. Stop and frisk was a popular practice used by law enforcement to racially profile black Americans. It goes back to the mindset that we, as black people, are seen as a group and not individual human beings. Therefore, if one person commits a crime, we are all guilty until proven innocent, but I still believe I could have a positive impact as a police officer.

My dream of becoming a police officer changed when one night, my friends and I were driving to a bowling alley in Bronx, New York. As we were getting out of the car to enter the bowling alley, my friends and I, without warning, were pushed against the car by four undercover white police officers. We were all illegally searched by the officers and asked the typical questions. Do you have drugs on you? Do you have guns in your possession? The officers then searched our car, found nothing, and simply left, stating this was a "mistake in identity". We were left afraid, embarrassed, and angry, knowing that our rights were violated. Moreover, our human dignity was violated, particularly because we were all law-abiding citizens.

This experience was ironic because my curriculum during the fall semester in college was about Probable Cause, Fruit of the Poisonous Tree, and Reasonable Suspicion. I quickly realized that Probably Caused or Reasonable Suspicion did not exist in this situation. The only cause that existed was our skin color. This was around the same time four New York City police officers fired 41 shots at unarmed Amadou Diallo, with no criminal record, killing him in the doorway. As a young black male, being stop and frisk simply because of my skin color, I felt lucky to escape that ordeal with my life. I later concluded that the "ideals" I was learning during my studies about the rule of law didn't apply to everyone.

I became enraged thinking about how many black law-abiding Americans have been mistreated by the inequity in the justice system. At that moment, it became clear to me that there are two systems of law. Depending on your skin color, in one system, you are innocent until proven guilty. Moreover, in the other system, you are guilty and must be proven innocent. I now know that I was judged by the latter.

In predominantly black communities, citizens are "policed" by law enforcement, but in white communities, law enforcement is there to serve and protect its citizens. I was so frustrated and angry at the hypocrisy of the "justice system" and how "un-just" it is to people of color. Therefore, I withdrew myself from the criminal justice program. I could not be a part of a career that oppresses people based on their skin color, economic status, and stereotypes.

The following semester, I transferred to St. John's University where I decided to major in legal studies. While attending St. John's University, I developed a love for sociology and the history of race in the United States. Four years later, I graduated from St. John's University with my bachelor's degree with honors. In other word, I was an honor student.

During my studies, I realized that as immigrants, we don't appreciate the sacrifices of millions of African Americans, who, through blood, sweat, and tears, fought to afford us this opportunity. We (immigrants) are benefiting and prospering from the pain and struggle of the black American people. We enter the United States better prepared to get ahead and take advantage of the opportunities to advance our careers.

We (immigrants) are not emotionally tied to the history of black people in the United States. Further, we were not subjected to sustained oppressive attacks against our humanity like African Americans. Therefore, it is much harder for African Americans to overcome the obstacles purposefully set in our way.

The tendency of many immigrants moving to the United States is to look down on African Americans as if to say they have all these opportunities living in the United States but are not taking advantage of them. However, they have never stopped to think about what it would be like to live with the people who stripped you of your humanity. To be villainized by your oppressors. A people stripped of their nationality, pride, purpose, and humanity.

Some immigrants fail to understand the impact this type of oppression has had on people. How do you pick up the pieces of a life when it is so utterly broken? African Americans carry deep wounds within their soul that must be healed for them to become whole.

I began to consider the resolve of the African Americans that they did not become terrorists seeking revenge for their pain—all they are asking for is equal justice under the law. The crazy thing is that when African Americans gain any victory, every immigrant living in the United States benefits. In a way, you could speculate that immigration hurts the progress of the African American people.

When I surrendered my life to the calling of Jesus at the age of twenty, I made the decision to forgive those police officers so that I could be free to become who God called me to be. Knowing in Jesus Christ, there is no unforgiveness and hatred. The scripture says, "Love your enemies and pray for those who persecute you, so that you may be sons of your Father who is in heaven; for he makes his sun rise on the evil and on the good and sends rain on the just and on the unjust." (Matthew 5:44-45)

Freedom a Call to Healing

When we are wronged, we often tend to hold on to the hurt, but we must surrender it and release the offender so that we can find the healing we need to move forward.

Chapter 3
Unresolved Scars from Our Past will Affect Our Future

And there was delivered unto him the book of the prophet Esaias. And when he had opened the book, he found the place where it was written, the Spirit of the Lord is upon me, because he hath anointed me to preach the gospel to the poor; he hath sent me to heal the brokenhearted, to preach deliverance to the captives, and recovering of sight to the blind, to set at liberty them that are bruised, to preach the acceptable year of the Lord. And he closed the book, and he gave it again to the minister, and sat down. And the eyes of all of them that were in the synagogue were fastened on him. And he began to say unto them, this day is this scripture fulfilled in your ears. (Luke 4:17-21)

In 2012, the Lord impressed upon the need to pray for the African American community. I felt the need to pray against the spirit of oppression that was being felt in the community. The shedding of innocent people on the streets, the issue of income inequality, the broken home, and the increased numbers of incarceration. The injustice in the school system and communities of the United States of America sent me to my knees.

People of color continue to struggle with the breakdown of the family structure, and this can be traced back to centuries of slavery, mass incarceration of black men, and poverty. During my research, I came to discover that approximately 34.4 percent of Black men were married in 2021, compared to 28.6 percent of Black women. For Whites, 55.5 percent of men and 52.4 percent of women were married. More than 48 percent of all Black women and 51.1 percent of Black men had never been married.

According to government statistics, approximately 71% of black babies are born to unmarried mothers today. The issue of fatherlessness is a direct contributor to poverty, crime, a feeling of worthlessness, and loss of hope. Our young men are lured to the streets to find a sense of purpose, and our young women are left with the burden of becoming single parents. Imagine the same destructive cycle continuing generation after generation, and no one ever stops to ask why. Forgetting that we and our children are always one bad decision away from the new form of slavery—the prison system.

I believe the mass incarceration of black men is directly tied to the issue of fatherlessness and America's greed for cheap labor in the prison-industrial complex. In the prison system, slavery was never abolished. Genuine rehabilitation was never the intention of the prison system; the goal of the prison system was another way to control and regulate black people.

For over four centuries, the United States has developed a dependency and value for free labor, and prisons allow this practice of devaluing human beings to continue. I recently watched a story on television of a black male who, while incarcerated, spent years in prison battling wildfires throughout the United States. As an inmate, he was pulling wealthy Americans and their families from burning homes. Upon his release from prison, he went and applied for a role to do what he loved but was declined due to his criminal record.

He was brokenhearted because, over the years while in prison, he became an expert at fighting wildfires. He was good enough while incarcerated because of his low human value. For example, I learned that Inmates serve as firefighters battling wildfires throughout the United States, and they earn $529.25 annually vs. a non-inmate-based salary of $57,000 per year, not including overtime.

I believe this is the reason that many issues affecting the black community coming out of slavery, Jim Crow, and segregation have never been addressed. We were doomed to fail; it was either sink, swim, or learn to swim if you were lucky. Naturally, many of our people learn to swim, some are barely keeping their head above water, and a segment has been drowning for decades. Therefore, the dysfunction and community-destroying habits are continually repeated generation after generation, not realizing the root causes and that we have the power to change course.

In addition, if we continue to choose not to change and embrace our God-given freedom and worth, the prison system is always waiting to gladly welcome us back to where our people started their journey in the United States—in slavery.

Many of our communities throughout the United States need a hard reset. To say what we are doing is not working in our favor, and we cannot continue to destroy the future of our children. The pattern of crime and violence must stop, and we must take responsibility for our actions. This has become a legacy where generation after generation are killing each other in our own communities. We are not safe in our own communities among our own people. Where do we find relief?

You are stressed when approached by law enforcement, and you are stressed living among your own people. Life is a survival game, and again, you sink, swim, or learn to swim if you are lucky. Unless our mindsets change and the value we place on each other, even if the gun laws were to change, the killing of each other would continue. We must look within for the solutions to change course, and it will not come from our favorite politician who only sees our value and worth when it comes to getting them elected.

When we allow Jesus Christ into our lives and submit to him, He begins the process of changing us from within. He can take a broken and hopeless situation—like my own life—and transform it into something new—I have heard countless testimonies of hardened criminals who gave their lives to Christ and live productive and impactful lives. I have seen firsthand the impact that Christ has on black families. It is such a beautiful thing to see black families strive, and this is observed in churches throughout the United States. People of color living for Jesus Christ and reaping the benefits of eternal life here on Earth.

The thing that makes a difference is when we accept Jesus into our hearts, He changes how we see our worth. He changes our thinking and gives us a sense of purpose. He gives us hope. It is such a wonderful feeling when we come to the realization that we are loved by an infinite God who sends his son into the world to die just for me in my worst condition. He died for us with no pre-conditions, knowing that we will reject him and all that He is offering us is a way of escape through his son Jesus Christ. Sometimes, we feel like we must fix ourselves before we come to God, but we are saved by grace through faith so that no one can boast. We are at our best as a people not in church, but in Christ Jesus.

It is so sad for me to say that we treat each other as a commodity and not as unique human beings. We are also treated as a commodity by law enforcement and those who need our money. In the eyes of many institutions throughout the United States, we are seen as a means to an end. We are not seen as human beings; we are judged by our perceived actions and by the actions of a few.

The I Have a Dream speech by Dr. Martin Luther King is far from being fulfilled because we are still judged and devalued on the basis of our color, except for our votes and purchasing power. It is time to change course and rethink who we are as a people.

It is sad that our young men still call and see each other as the N-word, and this is a big problem. We do not understand the power of words and how they shape our destiny. This goes back to our lack of worth and ignorance. Our young people need fathers and positive role models in their lives to show them another way. To show them that though this might be their reality, it is not normal for every generation within a family to be incarcerated. To show them that they have a choice and that selling drugs might be their reality on the street, but it is not the only option. There are opportunities available to become an entrepreneur, learn a trade, graduate college, and become whatever they set their minds to with dedication, determination, and guidance.

Devaluing and mistreating each other is destructive to our communities. This cannot continue into the next generation, and no politician is coming to help us. It is so heartbreaking to see black men give up on life, often due to poor choices or life circumstances that are lynching away the opportunities this great country affords to those who can take advantage of her bounties. We are lynching away our human life value and earning potential. We are lynching away the opportunities we have as fathers to impact the next generation. We are prone to take the easy path that leads to disaster and broken futures.

The systems of the United States are designed to label and limit those who fall prey to its injustice. Unfortunately, this has been our journey living in the United States, and it is a recipe for disaster. Therefore, so many of our communities are failing, and every year, more prisons are built to accommodate the next generation of black babies. How can we spend so much money as a country on forcing democracy on other nations and turn a blind eye to the continuing atrocities that are taking place in black communities throughout the United States?

We are committing a slow genocide against our own race. This must stop, and it requires divine intervention. We need a reset in our thinking, and we must do it for the next generation. It is time for us to redefine what it truly means to be black in America. We are overcomers. We are resilient. We are strong and beautiful people. We are a forgiving and merciful people. We have what it takes to live prosperous and fulfilling lives. We have the power to change course and fully participate in the American dream.

More churches need to get out of the four walls and go where the people are because we have something precious to offer that quenches the thirst of empty souls, and that is the word of the living God. They need to know that salvation is free, and it was brought and paid for by the blood of Jesus. We need to go where there is a need because truly hurting people are not walking through the church doors unless someone invites them. The need is great, and Jesus Christ calls us to become fishers of men for this very season we are living in today.

"Father, in the name of Jesus, I cry out to you because your creation and the people of African descent that you have created in your image and likeness are self-destructing in the cities and neighborhoods throughout the United States. We need your divine intervention to save us from the cancer within. We do not know how to change course or where to start, but I know that you can, and believe that you will, begin the process today with a little spark.

We need your help. You have kept our ancestors through their darkest hours, and I am asking you today, Sunday, November 6, 2022, for a revival within the black communities. I am asking for a new renaissance in the streets of the black ghettos, in the edges, alleys, under the bridges, and in the prisons where you find our people barely keeping their heads above water or drowning. I ask this in Jesus' name. Amen."

Chapter 4
The Failing Education System

The public school system is failing our children because the school cultures and environments are not conducive to learning and teaching. The fighting of cultures within the school system does not promote individuality and creativity. Instead, it promotes bullying and fights, and it's destroying the hope and self-esteem of our children. The public school culture, in many ways, mirrors a prison. Our children are wasting away their potential and youth. The pipeline to the prison system is in full effect, but we must work to limit its prey.

The hallways of the schools that should be filled with laughter, community, and fun are filled with anger and violence. Our children lack a sense of purpose, and they are filled with self-hate and pent-up anger. The problems within the broken homes of America are spilling over into the classrooms.

The school administrators and teachers are burnt out and overwhelmed because they feel powerless to meet the challenges within their schools. They spend more time breaking up fights and dealing with issues that have nothing to do with nurturing the dreams of today's children. Our children are not being motivated to learn, and they are being broken and pulled into despair and hopelessness. Every day, we send our beautiful children to the schools like sheep among wolves.

The children are bored and uninspired because they feel monitored. Many of the programs like sports and other activities have been taken out of the schools. Social media networks are destroying our children because they're negatively influencing them and are contributing to the destruction of the school culture and the way students treat each other. Negative social media trends are played out every day in the hallways and cafeterias of our schools.

Our children are failing because school is no longer a safe place to learn.

The schools have become a battleground and a social experiment. Something needs to be done to rebuild and reform the culture within our public schools. It's no wonder teachers who have a passion for teaching are quitting. There needs to be a reset in how we are thinking about learning and maybe the current model is outdated.

I recently watched a story on the Dr. Phil TV Show, in which he discussed how the education system is failing Americans and that the average high school student graduates with a 6th-grade reading level. At that moment, it occurred to me again that the issues we face as a community only matter at large when everyone is affected.

For over a century, our people have been complaining about the inadequate education that black children have been subjected to throughout this nation. The response is usually a deafening silence and inaction. As parents, we must teach our children to value education and challenge them to dream. We must push them to always give their best and teach them the importance of being their unique self and not compromising who they are to fit in and be accepted.

Reported in 2021, a Baltimore high school student failed all but three classes over four years and almost graduated near the top half of his class with a 0.13 GPA. Tiffany France, the mother of the failing student, thought her son would be receiving his diploma from Augusta Fells Savage Institute of Visual Arts in June. However, she was surprised to discover that he was being sent back to the ninth grade to start over.

France's son failed twenty-two classes and was late or absent 272 days over his first three years of high school. Only one teacher requested a parent-teacher conference, but France said that didn't happen. Despite this, her son still ranked 62nd in his class out of 120 total students.

The inadequate education system in black communities tends to function mostly as a daycare. The public school system works hand in hand with law enforcement and provides a projection for how many prisons are to be built.

Instead of the school system investing in developing and tapping into the talents and skills of our young people, the approach is more geared towards simply keeping them off the streets and curbing negative behaviors by being "watched"—just like in the prison system. The tentacles of racism can be seen throughout the education system and its deliberate efforts to limit others while elevating those it chooses.

The purpose of getting an education—if you are a logically thinking, normal person—should be to help all children fulfill their gifts and grow up to become law-abiding citizens. In addition, create trade schools for those who are not academically inclined. Instead, our children of color are desperate for knowledge, a sense of purpose, and hope. They need the hope that they will make it out of their current struggles and feel a part of the American dream. It is obvious that the education system in the United States is not equal and fair. The school system in the United States is deliberately segregated by those in positions of power.

The tool that is used to keep the U.S. schools segregated is zoning laws, and if you live in a predominantly black community that pays the same property taxes as your neighboring white community, the schools are terrible and lack resources. Even if you move into a white community that has middle-class black people when too many black people are attending predominantly white schools, there is always a reason for rezoning your children back to predominantly black schools outside of your zip code, and the excuses never make sense. Or you are fighting with the school district to keep your children out of special education, and unfortunately, this is a daily practice. Therefore, we need to wake up and fight for our children by getting involved in our local schools and local governments.

The oppressors have rewritten the stories of history, and they have moved on with their generational wealth. Many black people are left carrying the issues from the dark history of America that you would think did not exist. They embrace history when they are being glorified but deny history when the light is shined on their wicked and demonic deeds. Moreover, for decades it was hidden that institutionalized racism is still alive, well, and practiced throughout the United States. Many of the rights our ancestors died to secure are gradually and secretly being stripped away (voting rights).

The system is counting on a percentage of our children giving up on their dreams and accepting the lies that they will never make it. They feel worthless and give up hope. Therefore, the high school dropout rate for black males is 41%. In the modern United States of America, 41% of black males will not graduate high school, and no one seems to care. In the 2022 mid-term election, we see so many political campaigns running advertisements about the issues of crime and violence in the U.S. Yet, it is not breaking news that 41% of males will fall through the cracks and not graduate high school.

An analysis of 2018 U.S. Census Bureau data from the Education Trust found that nationally, only 26.5% of black men hold a college degree, compared to 44.3% of white men. Higher education leaders should respond to the most current enrollment declines among black men with "tremendous concern—and robust, multidimensional strategies," he said. "When the data tells us that we have a problem that is racialized and gendered, the solutions to that problem have to be racialized and gendered," Curry said a rash of campus recruitment and retention initiatives targeting these students can't make up for the thousands of black male students who fall through the cracks. He wants to see more systemic institutional changes that lead to "whole-school transformation."

I have not seen a black or white politician focus their campaign on fixing the black male school dropout rate, which will reduce crime and increase the earning gap. Instead, the solution for us is always to increase funding for law enforcement and build more prisons. If you were a child living in the inner cities of the U.S., would you feel hopeful and optimistic about life?

President Biden will ensure that no child's future is determined by their zip code, parents' income, race, or disability. Invest in our schools to eliminate the funding gap between white and non-white districts and rich and poor districts. There's an estimated $23 billion annual funding gap between white and non-white school districts today, and gaps persist between high and low-income districts as well.

Our young people are bombarded with images in the media that reinforce the concept that being black is criminal. The things that make us unique and special as a people get lost in how the media portrays us as inferior and sub-human beings. These images try to justify why the black race does not deserve freedom but instead should be monitored and controlled by law enforcement. These images feed white fear and quench their guilt. These images are further used by elected officials to stoke the fear of white people that the zombies are coming to take over their communities and that women and children are not safe. It is no wonder why when we move into white communities, there is an exodus shortly.

Mental illnesses are plaguing the black community, and trauma upon trauma is being inflicted by black-on-black violence and law enforcement, who are being paid from the taxes we pay to the government. We have yet to experience the true promise of freedom and liberty for all. We deserve the unalienable rights connected to the promise that all mankind is created equal; that right was not given by man but by almighty God. Our children want to believe that their dreams to prosper are relevant, attainable, and real.

It breaks my heart that so many innocent black people are killed by the police because they fear for their lives. Yet so many white mass murderers are arrested and put on trial. Something about this, to me, does not make sense. On one hand, you are killing people because you fear that they have a gun, and you are arresting mass murderers who you know have a gun.

The issue is so systemic that even though we march and demand change, it continues to happen. Police shooting of unarmed black people has become a way of life, and the justification is that their life was threatened. An unarmed black person is physically abused by police or shot to death in routine traffic stops. Young black Americans feel left out of a constitution that they believe should treat all lives the same and should protect the rights of all Americans. However, it always seems to fall short when it comes to the rights of black Americans.

Chapter 5
Bring Back the Good Old Days

On March 15th, 2024, I had a dream about a rich businessman who hates black people. The dream starts with him blaming a black person for stealing his credit cards. The Lord revealed to me in the dream that his credit cards weren't stolen, but they were stuck in the parking meter because he did not know how to operate the machine and broke it.

I could hear the businessman telling another white gentleman about how much he despised people of color; I then walked into the office to tell him that he had left his credit cards in the parking meter and that it was not stolen. The white gentleman he was talking to asked him, if every black person was a criminal, why would he return your credit cards? Moreover, it was not surprising to me that he dismissed the question as if he was being attacked.

The generosity I displayed gave me access to the evil schemes of this businessman as I continued to follow behind the white male. Though I was walking with the men, it was as if I was invisible to them. He began again to talk about how much he hates black people. They went into a conference room and began reviewing the blueprints for the evil plan that the businessman had for America.

The second gentleman was shocked to look at the blueprint and hear the businessman's new design to recreate America into a white utopia. The plan was to evict people of color from all cities and towns that they deemed desirable, regardless of their economic status. The plan was to move them out of the north side of the cities back to the south side.

The scheme is so elaborate that if a person of color goes into a store on the north side of town to shop, their purchase would be declined because the debit or credit is tied to their zip code. I could see whites making purchases, and everything gets processed as expected, and a black person tried to make the same purchase, but it was declined due to your zip code.

I started taking pictures of everything and recorded the conversation. They became aware that I saw their evil scheme to displace people of color. The businessman started to demand that I turn over my phone to him and that he would call the police. I could see police cars pulling up outside. I ran to the police officers to try to beat them to the lies they would tell them about me.

I started yelling that this man had a plan to recreate a white utopia in the United States and to create a new form of segregation. I yelled I have proof, and I am going to sue this company for discrimination. Next, I knew they started chasing after me to gain possession of my phone, and I woke up from my sleep.

There is a deliberate effort today throughout the States to take powers and protections from the Federal Government and give them back to the States. We are seeing at an alarming rate that states are doubling their efforts to chip away at the basic rights of African Americans, such as our right to vote and many others. History tells us that the motivation of those pushing this agenda is to restrict the rights and privileges of non-white citizens.

The primary motivation is the racist undercurrent of this society that has never been addressed. The protection that non-white citizens have enjoyed in the United States over the past 50 years is typically gained from the actions of the Federal Government and the courts, not from the state legislators. The attempt to disfranchise non-white citizens to gain or retain power is taking place across the United States today by those who believe the power should reside at the state level and by the "people."

The system of injustices is so engrained in policing, local government, and other institutions that they have doubled down on protecting white privilege and do not care about how it affects others. I look at what's going on in Florida and the complete disregard of black citizens who pay taxes in Florida. I find it disturbing that America is moving backward into the dark history of pre-Civil Rights practices in broad daylight before our very eyes.

State governments are not hiding their intentions anymore to protect white privileges; they are trampling on the rights that our ancestors fought so hard to secure. The sad part is that they are getting away with those practices because the Supreme Court is a sympathizer, and this was the reason they fought so hard to gain a judicial majority.

State leaders are moving forward with their destabilizing and oppressive agendas because when they are signing policies about anti-wokeness into law, there are black Americans behind them in the audience on center stage participating in the celebrations. We always seem to be in the photo-op when our freedoms are at stake, validating the agenda of those who working to limit our opportunities.

There is always that black person who contradicts our current reality and struggles. You can still see the "slave catcher syndrome" at play with black people who are willing to sell out their own race for a few dollars. So often, we become the tool that is used to soothe the guilty conscience of white nationalism by being the mouthpiece to say exactly what they want to hear and further support their hatred.

The mindset of those who believe in white supremacy is that the past fifty years have colored America through education and through systematic improvements. The motivation in the right-wing movement is to reverse the course of the coloring of America and strengthen historical white principles and values. One of the tactics to achieving this agenda is to control educational materials, because what you read helps to shape your worldview. These were the same schemes used to keep our ancestors in bondage and intellectual darkness for centuries.

It is not about making white children feel guilty; that is just a cover and talking points to justify their hatred. The goal is to keep white children from being tainted in how they see the world and embrace their true heritage. The heritage of whites did us a favor by taking us out of Africa and introducing us to the Americas. The heritage that Christopher Columbus discovered the world. They were losing their grasp on how to preserve whiteness. If you keep the factual African American history out of schools and you only teach the whitewashed American history, in their minds, they are preserving the next generation. The evil within it all is that you are protecting white children from "guilt" while crushing the hopes and dreams of black children, and as usual, they are the causality of white privilege.

The generations of post-civil rights are still pressing forward while seeing the "I Have a Dream speech" by Dr. King challenged like never before in this generation. The effects are taking a toll on our communities while our leaders are afraid to speak up and seek the necessary resources to truly help our communities deal with the lingering effects of slavery and the lack of opportunities for our youths.

It is very difficult to change the mind and consciousness of a person to empathize with your pain, a pain they have never experienced. Also, to have them acknowledge the scars they have caused, especially if it puts them in an unfavorable light and exposes the darkness in the heart of mankind for gain. It is far easier for them to convince themselves that they have done nothing wrong and that the "privilege" they are enjoying is because of hard work rather than a system that was set up to purposefully advance them by systematically oppressing others.

Moreover, it is even more difficult to admit the wrongdoing of the Forefathers of America if doing so, leads to the "leveling of the playing field," which would result in real "justice for all". It is a fact that some believe that slavery was a "necessary evil" to build the U.S. economy and its industries. In turn, this mindset eliminates empathy and feelings of guilt. It further desensitizes their minds from understanding that this system of slavery has had a detrimental, long-lasting, & sustained effect on not just those who directly experienced it but on multiplied generations thereafter.

When discontentment is expressed about how African Americans are treated and the lack of equity. We are seen as lazy and complainers who are essentially stuck in a perpetual victim mentality. The thoughts against us are hostile and indifferent. Statements such as just "pick yourself up by your bootstrap," which means doing something without any outside help, further desensitize others from truly understanding the frailty of human nature and its tendency to break under extreme pressures. It is far easier to say "they" should be satisfied with the opportunities they have now and the gains they have made and simply move on.

In the history of America, other human beings seem to get the empathy to mourn, acknowledge, and build memorials after a trauma occurs in their lives. All except the black race. We have experienced sustained trauma mentally, physically, emotionally, and spiritually in the Western Hemisphere that lasted well over four hundred years. Even after slavery, systems such as Jim Crow, segregation, and the systematic racism of today. Our people were expected to just pick up the pieces of life, adjust, and live as law-abiding citizens. We were expected to live in self-denial with multiple generations worth of pain and physiological programming, as if the scars we are carrying are healed or just don't exist.

Our trauma was to remain on the inside of us and eat away at us just like a cancer. It is too painful for us to release it and risk damaging the image of our oppressors. Therefore, the memories of pain & abuse passed down by our ancestors still reside on the inside of us at the level of our DNA. The pain is essentially destroying us from the inside out and the people around us. We are carriers of pain caused by centuries of oppression. Still, there has been no real remedy to cure us of these ills.

It often appears that many people in our community have given up on life. Many in our communities feel paralyzed, powerless, and left out of the American dream. Some feel worthless and hopeless because they feel oppressed. This inequality seems to be clearly indicated by the frequent violation of our constitutional rights through stop-and-frisk, as well as other measures used by law enforcement to control the black community through fear and intimidation while it acts as an extension of white supremacy. I always wonder why those who oppose our freedoms believe so strongly in law and order. It puzzles me sometimes of the devotion of those who believe in preserving the status quo and their devotion to law enforcement.

There is a silent war raging in American and Western countries because the freedom and equity we seek is perceived as an attempt to reduce their opportunities. Even though laws ended public discrimination several decades ago, the heart of America did not repent of its atrocities against the black race. In recent years, the hatred and vitriol that we (black people) thought only existed in our minds or just in a few (white) Americans we are seeing on a much larger scale. We are realizing the impact of the "system" and how it was set up to oppress some for others to truly succeed.

Instead of the benefactors of American privilege realizing their wrongs and attempting to change them so they are never repeated, they became silently enraged and callous. Equality "feels" to some like reverse oppression, and they further despise it because it was forced on them by law. Therefore, their hearts have not changed. Secretly, they have been scheming for decades on how to keep and strengthen their privileged positions.

We are prisoners of war because we are still experiencing psychological trauma that has continued for over four hundred years in the United States. One of the struggles we face as a people is from the memories of dark scars engrained within our minds and souls. The constant violation of our constitutional freedoms by those we entrust to protect them and the blatant disregard of the impact on current and future generations leaves me speechless.

The struggle of our people is systematic racism and the trauma that is infecting our communities. How do you set free a gift that has been wrapped and sealed for over four hundred years? How do we break free from our present battle when it often seems imaginary?

The ghost of post-slavery has set limits for how far we can climb. This holds us back from taking meaningful steps forward. We find ourselves in a place where we discover that we are prisoners of our minds and thoughts. Physically, we move around and do the things that appear normal. However, if we begin to open our minds and read the script of our journey, we will realize that we are walking in mud. Walking in mud is a slow and tedious process that often feels like the American journey and the struggle for true and lasting equality. The war continues and it appears all hope is lost. However, God, through His son, Jesus, has orchestrated a divine way out.

Oh, that wretched man that I am! Who shall deliver me from the body of this death? For the good I would do I do not, but the evil which I would not, I that I do. (Roman 7:24)

Jesus Came to Free the Captives

Jesus came to set the captives free. The people of Israel cried out for a savior to deliver them from their bondage. God, the Father, answered by sending His only begotten Son. God sent his Son into the world to relate to the common man. He could have been born in a palace; instead, He was born in a lowly manger. He also died a shameful death on our behalf.

He was beaten, separated from the Father, and abandoned by His disciples when He needed them most. Jesus died and suffered for our brokenness. He was rejected for our shame. He was mocked, discredited, scorned, and despised so that we could be freed from the bondage of a sinful life. He was stripped of His humanity and identity and hung on the cross for sins He did not commit so we can all be saved.

The healing and deliverance of our people must start with the people of God. We are redeemed and set apart. We are a chosen generation called to go into the highways and the by-ways to bring God's people back to the foot of the cross so that the process of lasting healing and deliverance can begin to take place. African Americans need the blood of Jesus so that widespread healing and deliverance can be ushered into the broken and hurting people.

God has a purpose for each person, and this includes the black American. One of the struggles we encounter is the ability to be able to connect to where we are. We often do not feel like true

American citizens. Although we all realize life is fleeting, we, more than others, seem to live life on a temporary basis. There is a lack of planning for the future. There is a lack of investment in the development of our young people, which stems from a temporary mindset. A mindset that is not fully convinced that America is "home" and that this is where we truly belong. This "temporary" mindset causes us to "survive" instead of "thrive".

Therefore, we tend to use money or things of value to validate our self-image and sense of accomplishment. There are many things we are connected to as we search for our identity. For example, sports, education, and careers. God wants to change our mindsets from being connected to "things" as our identity and become connected to Him, identifying with Him.

God created us to be free in Him and through Him. Every emotional pain we felt was nailed to the cross. Every suffering we endured was nailed to the cross. Our identity was nailed to the cross.

Our healing and deliverance from mental illnesses were nailed to the cross. All our hopes and desires for the future were nailed to the cross. Generational curses of self-destructive behaviors and mindsets were nailed to the cross.

The hope of a new future and a new beginning comes from a relationship with Christ, not with things, money, or titles. Everything we need to be whole is in Jesus Christ. Our identity is in Jesus Christ. We did not choose Him; He chose us and appointed us to bear much fruit (John 15:16). The branches that need to be pruned are destructive thinking, unforgiveness, fear to cry out for help, resentment, pride, self-hatred, poor self-image, addictive behaviors, idolatrous hearts, and the shedding of innocent blood through murder and abortion.

"For God so love the world that he gave his only begotten son, so that whosoever believe in Him should not perish, but have everlasting life. He did not come into the world to condemn the world, but that through the world might be saved" (John 3:16-17).

Chapter 6
Our Mental Fortitude

We have been conditioned as a people to hate what we look like, doubt our abilities, and accept the crumbs of society. Black Americans face numerous obstacles to achieving high levels of psychological well-being. Overcoming self-doubt and the feeling of inferiority is a daily decision for people of color.

Every day, we get up and make the decision to put one foot in front of the other and face the feeling of self-doubt—always feeling like we must prove our worth and sense of belonging. Pushing ourselves to go beyond our fears and comfort zones so that we can remove the barriers for our children so that what was abnormal to us is normal to them.

We make the decision to move into communities and accept roles in our careers where we do not feel welcome or wanted, but we push ourselves to overcome our limitations so that our children can stand on our shoulders instead of starting all over again. These are decisions we make every day despite self-doubt and fear. Being black in America sometimes feels like you don't get the freedom to mess up, and you often feel like a performer who must be perfect on every attempt. You feel judged and stigmatized. You must prove yourself to those in charge until they decide that you can be trusted.

Being black in America is a full-time job within itself, knowing that you are not wanted and that your presence may offend others. Yet we push away those feelings of self-doubt and do what we must do to survive and compete in this competitive world.

We often feel we are under a microscope, and sometimes, we find it very hard just to relax. We live in a state of constant stress because every day, we must show up and prove ourselves all over again. Though we are making decisions based on what's best for us and our families, we feel like we are carrying the weight of the community on our shoulders. The way we perform in a certain role may open the door for others to be welcomed or close the door of opportunity for others.

Being black in America carries weight and pressures. You feel like a child living in a home where you do not feel welcome and cannot be your authentic self. Walking into certain stores to shop knowing that you will be followed. Getting pulled over by law enforcement strictly because of the car you are driving. Always feel like you must prove your innocence and state of being.

Being black in America requires determination, resilience, and courage. Every day, we are creating a new normal for us and our families. Showing up at the community pool or the hot tub, knowing that it will be empty shortly after you arrive, we press on to create a sense of normalcy for our children. Walking into certain restaurants with all heads turning the moment you arrive, and you will wait extra-long to be served and acknowledged; yet we press on to create that sense of normalcy for our children.

Accepting and loving oneself is tied to a sense of belonging and self-worth. For us, as a people, to overcome self-doubt and feelings of inferiority, we must first accept that they exist. The U.S. is marked by sharp racial divisions in who has access to economic and social resources.

These divisions are the result of our country's history of racial stratification—the process by which laws are created, institutions are shaped, and policies and norms are enforced such that dominant racial groups maintain and improve their positions relative to other racial groups. Racial disparities in life expectancy and incidences of sickness are some of the most important consequences of racial stratification.

We must take the time to talk to our children about our experiences so that they are prepared to function and strive. If not, they will carry the frustration and anger, not knowing where it came from or how to cope. Too often, our children are left with anger and frustration because they feel oppressed and do not know how to verbalize their feelings or if what they are feeling is even real.

Given the implied pressures we feel as grown-ups living in America, even more so, our children do not fully understand that we live in a world where we are judged strictly based on our skin color. We owe it to them so that they understand why, as parents, we must push them to do things that they are uncomfortable with so that they are not limited by their environment. They have the God-giving abilities to achieve whatever they aspire to accomplish with hard work and the support we provide. Letting them know that the difference between success and failure is the opportunities that you are afforded. These are the reasons we push ourselves to overcome our limitations to create new opportunities for them.

I find that the best way to overcome self-doubt and fear is to accept who I am in God, knowing that he died to set a captive like me free from all worries and fear, knowing that my worth lies within Him. It is just a great feeling knowing that God is not like man. He sees you at your very worst and loves you despite it. Knowing Jesus Christ as my Lord and Savior has helped me to manage and overcome my self-doubt.

"Incline your ear, and come unto me: hear, and your soul shall live; and I will make an everlasting covenant with you, even unto the sure mercies of David." (Isaiah 55:3)

In the history of America, other human beings get the empathy to mourn and build memorials after a trauma occurs in their lives, except the black race. We had a trauma in the Western Hemisphere that lasted over four hundred years and is still ongoing. One day, due to the perseverance and sacrifice of many, the law told us that we were free.

After slavery and segregation, our people were expected to simply pick up the pieces and move on with their lives as if nothing happened and everything was perfectly normal. It was like a movie, destruction everywhere, and suddenly everything returned to its normal and you are left wondering what just happened. We were told to move on and get over it as if the physical, emotional, and psychological trauma did not occur. We were expected to live in self-denial as if the scars we were carrying never really happened. It is only in our heads.

Despite our physical and psychological bondage, which resulted in scars being embedded into our very being, we still managed to limp forward. For many years, I have been burdened by the injustice that was done and is happening to my people. Instead of being provided with resources to assist local churches and other organizations with the training necessary to put the black race in a position to compete and strive in America, other destructive agents like drugs were placed in the community to thwart any positive progress. The black community was introduced to drugs, welfare, and project housing as "pacifiers" for pain and problems.

I remember having a dream in 2013, and the Lord showed me our ancestors as they were coming off the slave ships. He showed me that there were elements in their new environment that could have wiped out many of our ancestors, even as they were getting off ships. In the dream, there was a man who looked like he was from ancient biblical times guiding them. The man turned and said to me, "Do you remember me from thirteen years ago?" I thought about the question and discovered I had been a Christian thirteen years ago.

I saw the man in the dream ministering to our ancestors as they were working in the cotton fields. Then, I saw the Lord God Almighty seated on His throne with a bright light radiating from the throne, and I began crying profusely. The Lord showed me that even in our struggle for freedom, He was there to preserve and keep us just as He did our ancestors. God reminded me in the dream that just as He delivered our ancestors, He, too, had delivered me from the bondage of sin and death. He is able and willing to deliver us all if we cry out to him, our mighty deliverer.

Chapter 7
The Freedom We Seek

So do not fear, for I am with you; do not be dismayed, for I am your God. I will strengthen you and help you; I will uphold you with my righteous right hand. 11 "All who rage against you will surely be ashamed and disgraced; those who oppose you will be as nothing and perish. (Isaiah 41:10–11)

The freedom and validation we seek will not come from the U.S.; this would require divine intervention. It can only come from a relationship with our Lord and Savior Jesus Christ. We live in a world where order and structure have been created and shaped in the image and likeness of white supremacy. It was never intended for us as a people to get this far in the journey of freedom so quickly, given the lies that we have been told about our inabilities.

In addition, we must be re-educated that God is not a white person. If blacks were the dominant culture instead of whites, then everything good created would have been black and vice versa. Genesis 1:26 says, *"Then God said, let us make man in our image, according to our likeness."* If everyone in creation drowned in the flood except the family of Noah, where did the notion of white supremacy come from? It was not from God because we are all descendants of Noah. Who told people of European descent that they were superior? It was a lie from the pit of evil, and again, this was a scheme developed to become wealthy by controlling others. Colonize other human beings who value culture over material wealth. This was a scheme to kill and plunder the wealth of other human beings without feeling guilt and accountability. To my knowledge, no one has been held accountable for colonizing the wealth of so-called third-world nations while leaving its people broke and destitute.

God is spirit and can only be discerned spiritually. We are created in his image and likeness: body, soul, and spirit. Each of us human beings reflect the image of God. Our humanity was given by God, and it is not left up to the interpretation of the wicked and self-seeking man whose desire is to marginalize and enslave other human beings for power and economic greed.

The biggest threat to white supremacy is united blacks and diversity. The true freedom we seek must come from God because He cannot lie. If he lies, he will cease to be God. His words are unchanging, and his promises are sure. "Vengeance is mine; I will repay" (Hebrew 10:30). If we seek justice and truth from white America, they can always change the narrative when it's not in their favor.

The 14th Amendment gave us equal protection under the law. On the contrary, the Supreme Court in the Slaughterhouse Cases in 1873 ruled that "most of Americans basic civil rights were obtained through their citizenship in a state and the amendment did not protect those rights." The court drove a stake into the 14th Amendment, which made it legal for states to pass discriminatory laws against blacks.

Can you imagine the despair our ancestors felt? Having fought in wars for America's independence but was left out of the constitution. Who also fought in the Civil War to save the American Union while being denied their own human dignity. Finally, the country made good on its promise, and Congress passed the 14th amendment on July 9, 1868, granting them citizenship, and five years later, those rights were stripped away by the Supreme Court. This is another example of why we must be vigilant and not rest because legislation is passed in our favor. There is always a white resistance to reduce your victory when you least expect it. White resistance is typically driven by fear. Whenever the survival of white supremacy is threatened, like in January 2020, they can rewrite history and the laws to protect and preserve white supremacy.

The Freedom We Seek

We Must Remain Vigilant In our Struggle for Equal Rights

The Supreme Court on Tuesday, June 25, 2013, struck down a section of the Voting Rights Act, weakening a tool the federal government has used for nearly five decades to block discriminatory voting laws. In a five-to-four ruling, the court ruled that Section 4 of the Voting Rights Act is unconstitutional.

On Monday, January 28, 2022, the high court said it would take up a pair of cases that challenge the use of race as a factor in undergraduate admissions at Harvard University, the nation's oldest private college, and the University of North Carolina, the nation's oldest public state university.

The U.S. Supreme Court will once again revisit the legality of affirmative action in higher education after last upholding the decades-old precedent in 2016. Some studies suggest the policies—which consider race as one of many factors when reviewing applicants to further a diverse student body—have had a profound effect on opportunities for minority applicants, which in turn, impact their job chances and careers. They suggest that stopping them not only decreases the number of Black and Latino students enrolling in colleges but also increases those of advantaged groups.

Those dedicated to white supremacy always play the long game. Long after we have moved on and begun adjusting to our new freedoms, as I have stated repeatedly, there is always resistance when we least expect it. The excuse is usually that society is more diverse, and those protections are no longer needed, and we always go along with it not thinking about the long-term ramifications. Fifty years after the passing of the Voting Rights Act, a group decided to sue, which brought it before the court, and the Supreme Court could not avoid living up to its reputation of undermining the rights and freedoms of blacks in the United States.

It's time for us to re-evaluate how we view the Supreme Court because when it comes to landmark cases that involve black people, white supremacists always use the court to their advantage. We cannot just look to Congress to pass laws knowing that at some point in the future, the Supreme Court will rescind the laws. When you look at history time and time again, after years of sweat, blood, and tears fighting for legislation in Congress that grants us equality and the rights we deserve, the Supreme Court often sides against us. We must stop only looking at just the Democrats and Republicans for the lack of systematic change in the United States. We also must blame the Supreme Court, which operates in the shadow while its rulings have long-lasting and life-changing effects.

As we are awoken to the fact that our strength lies in our collective ability to organize and hold politicians accountable who have taken oaths to preserve the status quo, it has become apparent that most white Americans are comfortable with the status quo because it is beneficial to their quality and way of life. For example, one of the primary causes of death in America is gun violence. At this moment, gun violence has not reached epidemic proportions for whites, where their quality of life is affected, and as a result, the laws against guns will not change at the Federal level.

Moreover, when opioid drug addiction did not reach epidemic proportions in white communities, it was criminalized and used as a tool against the black community, particularly against black men. On the contrary, when it reached epidemic proportions in white communities, it was no longer criminalized, but drug addiction was labeled a disease.

We had no idea the deep-seated dark truth about racism. Racism is necessary to preserve the white way of life. If you remove racism, then you will have no white privileges and a loss of the white advantages. They would be marginalized the same way blacks are today. They would be imprisoned the same way blacks are imprisoned. The quality of their education would deteriorate to the level of blacks because the resources would be somewhat equally given to all communities. Likewise, blacks would experience a greater level of prosperity and freedom. The truth is that racism unites Western Civilizations.

I believe the nail that holds Western Civilization together is racism, and one of the biggest threats is diversity. Diversity creates division within the white community, and they, themselves, become divided based on an evolving core belief that we are human beings as well and deserve the same protections.

It is imperative that we as a people look to God for our true freedom and liberty that we seek. The trend arising in this nation is tribalism, and if we look closely at the sign, the U.S. is in danger. To preserve white privilege, there are millions of people who would fight a civil war if that's what it takes to "Make America Great Again."

Therefore, at the point of desperation and the feeling of self-preservation, they will change the rules and laws that are not in their favor. For example, whenever mass murders are committed by white males—which is very frequent—these brutal acts carried out by white males are immediately labeled as mental illness by white politicians and the media. Have we ever stopped to ask why? They understand the power of labels, and if these white males are labeled terrorists, then white supremacist groups would be under the scrutiny of the FBI and law enforcement. It would also possibly tie their radicalization to white supremacy. Therefore, it is always the same script: mentally ill and lone wolf. Yet, these are the same people who will create commercials talking about crime and the need for tough law enforcement, but they only show you the face of a black male.

The faces of the mass murderers disappear in the night because they are mentally ill. I do agree that it takes a mentally ill person to kill another human, but this standard should not just apply to keep white males from being labeled by the justice system. Moreover, it is clear to me that crime has a face, and it matters who is seen as a criminal. Unfortunately, rightfully or unrightly, black males have become the posture child for crime and violence in Western Civilization. I believe this is done deliberately to keep white males from being labeled or stigmatized. It is also brainwashing because just fifty years earlier, these were the same people beating innocent blacks who were seeking basic rights. What happened to their vicious nature? It was whitewashed like everything else in history, and all we are left with is our imagination. There is a reason the justice system tries so hard to keep whites out of the prison system as it is currently constructed it was not made for them. It was created as an extension of slavery for black Americans.

In addition, if you look closely enough, you will realize that these individuals were radicalized by a white supremacist group, but those details are kept from the public. Moreover, if the same crimes were committed by a Muslim or a black person, they are either "Terrorists or Thugs". He who is in power controls the narrative, and that became very evident given what happened on January 6, 2020: Words and labels matter.

We must remember that laws and statutes do not change the hearts of people; they only force them to change their behavior and attitude, but most times, those very laws are forced upon them, and they find other ways to carry out their hatred. If the Ten Commandments given by God did not change the sinful hearts of human beings, then why do we expect a law to fix all our issues? The true freedom we seek can only come from a relationship and revelation of our Lord and Savior, Jesus Christ. Finally, if our ancestors did not look to a higher power other than themselves, it would have been impossible for them to survive the hardship of slavery and oppression for centuries.

Chapter 8
The Deception of the American Dream

Thus saith the Lord that made thee, and formed thee from the womb, which will help thee; Fear not, O Jacob, my servant; and thou, Jeshurun, whom I have chosen. For I will pour water upon him that is thirsty, and floods upon the dry ground: I will pour my spirit upon thy seed, and my blessing upon thine offspring: And they shall spring up as among the grass, as willows by the water courses. (Isaiah 44:2-4)

The system of capitalism is not meant for everyone to be successful. In some ways, before you were born, the opportunities you were born into have distinct advantages and disadvantages. The American dream reminds me of working a commission-paying job. There are no guarantees that you will be successful; it only offers you an opportunity. Quite frankly, it's counting on a large segment of people to fail, and those individuals who attain success become the role models for why attaining generational wealth is possible.

However, it does not tell us that most people who attempt to achieve the dream will fail or fall at different levels of the spectrum. A few at the top, a smaller segment in the middle, and a larger group who are making just enough to continue believing that if they just change a behavior, attitude, or habit, success is possible. Often, you give up feeling like a failure and that you do not measure up without realizing that the environment and the built-in barrier within the system affect your success. Together, those individuals at the top and the middle serve as the motivating factors for why everyone can make it if they only try. The uniqueness of capitalism is the opportunity it provides. Though we all have the same opportunities to succeed, based on the racial and socioeconomic background we are from, there are barriers that limit the attainment of the American dream.

Very deep social and economic inequities persist in the black community. Many Americans aren't aware of the magnitude of these entrenched problems. Black children are three times as likely as white children to grow up in poverty, and they are much more likely to remain there. Black Americans also face significant challenges in other areas that affect their quality of life and overall prosperity. Homeownership rates are stagnant among all black households and are falling for black millennials.

Voting rights have once again been put in jeopardy in ways that disproportionately affect minority communities, making it more difficult for black people to advocate for better policies. Significant racial disparities in health outcomes remain. There are few signs that these inequities will diminish soon or that market forces alone will address them. Bold economic policies will be necessary to improve the economic state of black America moving into the future, but the first steps are to recognize just what progress has been made and how much further we have yet to go.

We bought into the American Dream that if we work hard and strive, we will achieve the freedom, prosperity, and equality that it offers. Moreover, we spend our lives trying to live up to its ideals, only to realize that in its fullness, it cannot be fully attained. We discover that the system and the people who maintain and preserve their perception of us have not fully evolved. Even though we serve in the military, strive to be educated, and be good citizens—often, we fall short.

Once attaining your desired economic status, you feel like you have arrived and have achieved success. You begin to bask in the life, liberty, and the pursuit of happiness which are promised in the Declaration of Independence. You are disappointed to realize that we are still not fully accepted by a system that was never created for our enjoyment and pleasure.

For generations, we turn around and tell our children the same ideals of what makes you a productive and successful American.

Go to school and get a good education, which is true and necessary. Respect the authorities and say please and thank you. We were never told that what truly makes you an American is your skin color and your ability to assimilate. The fact that we do the things white Americans do does not fully qualify us, and because of our skin color, we are automatically labeled and quietly excluded.

When we are approached by law enforcement, they do not see a law-abiding person. Instead, they see our color and the stereotypes. Therefore, the laws we believe in and the reality we experience are always at odds with each other. For example, the law says, "Innocent until proven guilty," but the reality says, "You are guilty until proven innocent."

This is one of the reasons so many innocent black males are killed by law enforcement because before approaching and having a conversation with you, they have determined in their minds you are guilty of something. In addition, your very appearance triggers that mental alert that says "Danger," and that is the reason our men are killed unjustly by those who were hired to protect and serve.

Similarly, when we enter certain stores to shop and feel in our hearts and minds that we have attained success only to be followed around the store. It is well documented that whites steal just as much as black people or more, but they do not see us as individuals. Our color is the first thing that is viewed and judged.

The sad truth is that we are constantly reminded that the past is behind us, and we are the reason we fail in this nation. In doing so, they absolve themselves from all responsibilities and you are left to figure out the mess and disfunction. I believe we are the most resilient people ever to walk the face of the Earth. Regardless of how much we get knocked down and trampled underfoot, we always find a way to get back up.

Therefore, we work twice as hard subconsciously to prove to the whites that we are not like the rest of "them." In addition, as soon as you make a mistake, they are reminded that you are one of them and are treated accordingly. It is amazing to me that the very people who love individualism and freedom work very hard to label and treat others like a group instead of individuals.

As soon as we attain some level of success, we immediately leave our neighborhoods and move to the suburbs—trying to fully separate ourselves from "them." Not long after, we are reminded of the reality that whether we are in a black-populated area or in the suburbs, our children are faced with the same issues with law enforcement and the built-in barriers.

The system was designed to punish and keep "them" in order because we are unable to self-govern. You are reminded that even though you think you are one of the law-abiding citizens, we cannot change the color of our skin by which we are judged. It's important for us as people of color to realize that we are not fighting against white Americans but the ideology that they are superior and everyone else is inferior. Until that ideology is controlled or defeated, the freedom and success we seek on a large scale will not be fully realized.

Chapter 9
The Absolute Power of Law Enforcement

I [patroller's name], do swear that I will, as searcher for guns, swords, and other weapons among the slaves in my district, faithfully and as privately as I can, discharge the trust reposed in means the law directs to the best of my power. So, help me God. (Slave Patroller's Oath, North Carolina, 1828)

I am disheartened by the absolute power that law enforcement has when interacting with the black community. The unprofessionalism that is displayed during a minor infraction causes me to wonder if policing in America ever truly evolved from its original core beliefs. Even though the world is made aware of police brutality and the inhumane treatment of blacks in America via cell phone cameras. Instead of Congress and the Senate passing new laws to reform the way policing is done, things seem to be getting worse.

It has become a common occurrence for an unarmed black male, female, or youth to be gunned down by law enforcement because they thought the victim had a gun. You would think by now that this defense would cause alarm throughout every community in America because the standard for killing an innocent black person by law enforcement only requires a thought. I find it very difficult to understand that a trained professional is justified in taking an innocent life because of their own fear and bias. There is no burden of innocent until proven guilty, we always seem to get the short end of the stick. I believe this goes back to the very origin of law enforcement, that a black person is guilty until otherwise proven innocent, and this unwritten standard has not changed.

For years, my wife and I would watch the television show, Cops. I was always amazed by the compassion and understanding that law enforcement has for the majority of the race. Even when they were caught practicing prostitution and engaging in other criminal behaviors, they treated them with a sense of humanity. Sometimes, law enforcement would make the decision not to make an arrest because the person deserved another chance at life and prison was not the best situation for them. On the contrary, when law enforcement encounters a person of color, the role seems to be to keep us in check, and there is hardly any compassion or empathy. We are treated as if being a criminal is in our DNA, and when white people break the law, there must be a justifiable reason for the occurrence.

I was watching CNN recently as they were covering the mass shooting at the nightclub in Colorado, and they had a profile of the shooter that I find to be very offensive and disturbing. The reporter was covering the fact that his parents were divorced and other incidents that occurred in his life to justify the usual defense of mental illness. The goal is always to humanize the criminal if they are a white person.

On the other hand, there was an incident recently where police executed a no-knock warrant, and a black male sleeping in the living room was startled by what he perceived to be an intruder entering his home. He reached for his licensed firearm and was shot to death. Before the truth was ever made public, law enforcement did their best to criminalize this individual. They put out misinformation to smear and discredit the victim's character in the typical manner done to people of color.

I believe the motivation for this defense of mental illness is to brainwash the public by stating that a white person only commits crimes when they are mentally ill. They are covertly telling us that it is not in a white person's nature to commit brutal crimes and to be lawbreakers. They are telling us that a white person is inherently good, and I believe this influences laws and even how they are policed.

Oftentimes, I am left wondering where the disconnect is between policing the white community and engaging in the same criminal practices as people in the black community. It has become clear to me that the way you are policed is determined by how you are defined and labeled by the white majority. They most often received textbook policing standards—innocent until proven guilty. The brainwashing we have received from those in power and the media says, by nature, that a white individual is good and a black person is inherently bad. It's no wonder there is a divide in how the white communities and the black communities experience policing. In the white communities, the police are problem solvers versus being an oppressive force in the black communities.

I am further disturbed by white females who seem to believe that the police function as their personal bodyguards where they can act in a prejudicial manner towards a person of color and always seem to leverage the police as a weapon. I read a story recently where a white woman called the police on a nine-year-old black girl who was simply watering lantern flies. Why? The brainwashing says she is black and she must be doing something wrong. If they feel threatened by your presence, their first response is to call law enforcement.

Maybe they know something about law enforcement that we are not privileged to know. It would appear to me that law enforcement has an inherent responsibility to protect the interest and privilege of the frail and dainty white female. They seem to have a level of comfort and safety with law enforcement that the black community has never experienced. This belief that law enforcement will come to their protection, especially if a person of color is involved, seems to be traced back to the history of policing in America and racial stratification.

Racial stratification—the process by which laws are created, institutions are shaped, and policies and norms are enforced such that dominant racial groups (whites in the American context) maintain and improve their positions relative to other racial groups.

What is the norm?

- An authoritative standard: MODEL.

- A principle of right action binding upon the members of a group and serving to guide, control, or regulate proper and acceptable behavior.
- A pattern or trait is taken to be typical in the behavior of a social group.
- A widespread or usual practice, procedure, or custom.

I have seen countless stories where a black person is watering their gardens and a white person passing by who doesn't think you belong there, and you must be breaking the law. Their first inclination is to leverage their lifeline by calling law enforcement. Once law enforcement arrives, the burden of proof is removed from the person who called law enforcement to you now having to prove your right to exist on your own property. The brainwashing says you are black, you must have broken a law, or you are in the process of breaking a law.

When is it ever the responsibility of the white person who contacted law enforcement to prove that the call was not done out of bias and, in turn, issue a fine for wasting the resources of the local law enforcement unit? However, the mindset seems to be that if a white person calls law enforcement on a person of color, there must be a justifiable reason, and you must be guilty until they determine your innocence.

The history of policing can be traced back to the days of slavery in colonial America. In the South, where slavery was central to the economy, slave patrols, responsible for capturing runaway slaves and returning them to their masters, were the first unofficial police in America.

Considering how slavery itself was one of the most egregious treatments of mankind in human history, slave patrols were especially cruel in the ways they captured runaway slaves and punished them for their daring escapes. Slave rebellions were a constant threat to the economic status quo of the southern plantation owners, and slave patrols ensured that these owners were able to intimidate and punish any insurgencies or revolts.

In return, these wealthy plantation owners protected the interests of the slave catchers. This practice created a social hierarchy between the wealthy landowners at the top, the slave patrols separating the wealthy from the poor, and the slaves who were at the bottom of this hierarchy.

These slave patrols slowly morphed into policing units in charge of breaking up insurgencies that began to rise in the aftermath of the Civil War. When the Civil War ended, many colonists, especially Southerners, felt threatened by the population of freed African Americans, arguing that they would disrupt the social order. As a result, African American communities experienced an increase in violence committed against them in the form of police brutality. The Reconstruction Era, which came immediately after the Civil War, was a racially charged environment as the newly freed citizens attempted to live peacefully amongst their oppressors.

During the Reconstruction Era, cruelty was the policing style, and protecting the economic interests of the wealthy proved very beneficial to these units. Police were used to provide a sense of security for the white communities, keeping the black communities intimidated and segregated from the white population. Additionally, reconstructing the South after the war would require a lot of free labor and much of the reconstruction that took place was achieved through the enforced hard labor of the newly freed population, who were shortly enslaved again—this time through the prison system.

Known as the Jim Crow laws, several legislations were passed to keep the black and white communities segregated, and racist policies were put in place to target and imprison people of color. In part due to the loophole in the thirteenth amendment, which abolished slavery except as a form of punishment, policing centered around rounding up and arresting African Americans for violating the racist Jim Crow Laws, denying them their fundamental rights as human beings. Ironically, the loophole provided by the thirteenth amendment gave rise to today's prison industrial complex.

I believe law enforcement when practiced in an unbiased manner with accountability and transparency is necessary to maintain order in every community throughout the United States. Even with its many faults and shortcomings, law enforcement is necessary. However, when a group of people is treated differently solely based on their race and economic status, this should be alarming and unacceptable to everyone.

Chapter 10
The Great Divide

And if a household is divided against itself, that household will not last. So if Satan rebels against himself and is divided, he cannot last. That will be the end of him. "No one can go into a strong man's house and steal his property. First, he must tie up the strong man. Then he can go through the strong man's house and steal his property." (March 3:25-27)

The great divide in the United States has to do with maintaining the status quo or rejecting white supremacy. For the first time in American history since the Civil War, white Americans are divided, and at the core of the divide is what they value. You have those who value equality and believe the playing field should be level for all Americans, and to the contrary, you have those who believe in white Americans first.

To this day, Trump supporters believe that the election was stolen because Trump won the popular vote and electoral college; at its core, they sound crazy and deceived. However, in their eyes, most whites voted for Trump, and therefore, it was stolen. Blacks and other minorities are not included in their total. The election was stolen by blacks and "Woke" white Americans. To be "woke" politically in the black community means that someone is informed, educated, and conscious of social injustice and racial inequality, Merriam-Webster Dictionary states.

You would think that a country that celebrates freedom and the right to vote would celebrate the fact that there was a record turnout in the middle of a worldwide pandemic. The system worked because voting is a right given by Americans, and millions turned out to exercise their constitutional right. However, it created fear and terror of what was to come as America got more diversified and heightened the consciousness of those who were devoted to preserving white supremacy.

For the first time in 25 years of living in the United States, I am deeply concerned that we are in a very bad place as a country. The United States is rapidly declining, and the beacon on the hill it represented for decades has become dark. We are in a very dark place as a country, and a house divided against itself will not prosper. There is a decline in moral standards by those elected to the highest offices, which you would think would be the moral standard of the country.

In previous years, everyone in Congress and the Senate stood for the Constitution, but from this election, it is obvious that one party is trying to preserve democracy and American ideals. On the other hand, one party has forsaken the Constitution and human dignity but instead clearly stands for white supremacy.

To maintain power is to control the narrative. They have changed the voting laws that govern elections in Georgia and many other states. As the consciousness of most Americans is "Awoken," America is heading toward a full-out war against itself. There is a fraction of white Americans who embrace and acknowledge the wrongs of the past. On the other hand, a large segment feels like they are losing everything and that the country is being stolen from them.

For example, when Kyle Rittenhouse murdered two white Americans at the Black Lives Matter protest and injured two others, he was not arrested on the spot. Even though he had blood on him and was walking with a gun—because of his skin color, at no time was he seen as a threat to law enforcement. Though white Americans were killed, he was called a hero and liberationist. Why? He defended white supremacy and stood against everyone who bowed to diversity and inclusion, which is the greatest threat to the system.

The Bible says Satan is the father of all lies, and there is no truth in him (St. John 8:44). It is so baffling to me that tens of millions of people in this country will believe the lie that Trump won the election. It is important to note that a large segment of those claiming the election was stolen sees blacks and other minorities as invaders of America, and they do not recognize us as citizens. Those who voted for Trump are considered legitimate votes, and the rest of us are not. If you look closely at the cities that were audited for fraud, it is where a large number of blacks and other non-whites live. In many ways, the media is also to be blamed because they only care about ratings and money. We should understand that the media's responsibility is to report facts. For centuries, the media has been a part of the problem.

According to the Britannica, "white supremacy, beliefs and ideas purporting natural superiority of the lighter-skinned, or "white," human races over other racial groups. In contemporary usage, the term white supremacist has been used to describe some groups espousing ultranationalist, racist, or fascist doctrines. White supremacist groups often have relied on violence to achieve their goals." If we look back on what happened in the United States Capitol on January 6, 2020, this definition is spot on.

The United States of America is in a very dangerous position because millions of young white men are being radicalized on the premise that we invaders are taking away their country. The invaders are non-white immigrants who are migrating to the United States. At this very moment, while the rest of us are asleep and focusing on our daily lives, they are preparing for a civil war. The difference between the Civil War between the North and the South is that these people lived everywhere. They are your neighbors, and if you attend a diverse church, they sit beside you every Sunday; some are your pastors. They are in government, school boards, law enforcement, and the military. They are your children's schoolteachers, they are your co-workers, they are doctors, judges, and your friends at work.

Three retired US Army generals warned of an insurrection or even civil war if the results of the 2024 presidential election were not accepted by some in the military: former Major Gen. Paul Eaton, former Major Gen. Antonio Taguba, and former Brig. Gen. Steven Anderson made the warnings in an op-ed in The Washington Post on Friday. They wrote that they were "increasingly concerned" about the 2024 election and the "potential for lethal chaos inside our military."

The generals highlighted the "disturbing number" of veterans and active-duty members of the military that took part in the January 6 attack on the Capitol by Trump supporters—more than 1 in 10 of those charged had a service record. The military should also work to identify how misinformation spreads in the ranks. The generals also suggested that the Defense Department should "war-game" possible post-election scenarios to identify weak spots and put in place "safeguards." (Insider: Retired US army generals warn of insurrection or civil war in 2024 if rogue military units pledge loyalty to a 'Trumpian' loser by Alia Shoaib Dec 19, 2021, 6:12 AM)

We look at the situation, and it does not make sense. It's as if the veil has been removed, and all these things that we felt as people of color and have complained about for years are suddenly in the open. We are American citizens. We are here legally through the immigration system or by birth. We were brought here centuries ago, and this is our home. We are living in a different reality than the people who are devoted to protecting and preserving white supremacy. On one hand, we see diversity as a good thing, and that it creates opportunities for all people. We see it as the country finally living up to its founding principles and values. However, what we see as significant progress and opportunities, they see it as they are losing, and we are taking what belongs to them.

I am sure by now it is starting to make sense why these people are losing their minds against non-white Americans when you encounter them in the stores or when you are walking around your community. They often say that you don't belong and should go back to your country. They are accusing us of stealing from them, and they are quick to call the police to come to their defense. Until we know and embrace the reality of the times we are living in and hold the media, as well as political leaders, accountable for telling the truth, we are in great danger.

Barbara F. Walter, a civil war expert, said the US is closer to violent conflict than many think. She cites racial resentment among whites who believe black Americans or other minority groups are now getting unfair special treatment. She also points to Trump's focus on the grievances of working-class white people and his attempts to appeal specifically to those who feel they have lost something, as evidenced by his slogan, "Make America Great Again."

"Where is the United States today? We are a factionalized anocracy that is quickly approaching the open insurrection stage, which means we are closer to civil war than any of us would like to believe," Walter concludes.

Walter explains that a civil war today might look different than in the past. She points to specific examples of violence, like the extremist plot to kidnap Michigan Gov. Gretchen Whitmer and the insurrection at the Capitol, as indicators that at least some groups are already willing to move toward violence. (Business Insider: US is ‹closer to civil war than any of us would like to believe,› a leading expert on civil wars says in a new book Kelsey Vlamis Sat, January 22, 2022, 2:16 AM·4 min read)

We live in a period of darkness, and the only light that can drive the darkness from man's heart is the light of Jesus Christ. We need Jesus more than ever before as more and more people of this nation have forsaken their relationship with God and are worshipping conspiracy theories and lies. The world does not need love, it needs Jesus. There is no true and lasting love without Jesus because He is love.

We have taken him out of every area of society, not realizing that when we remove light from a room, darkness, dysfunction, division, and anarchy will take its place. This is not a time for us to fear, but it is a time for us to repent of our sins and turn to our Lord and Savior. It is a time for us to cry out to God to have mercy on the United States of America and to cry out for a revival to come upon the land. When God is not in the mix, we are left to our savage nature. The failure of man is everywhere, and we are witnessing the fall of a great nation. In the book of John, Jesus stated that he came to his own, and they received him not because man loves darkness more than they love the light. (John 1:11) We must look at this segment of society with empathy. Jesus said we should love our enemies. They are deceived into believing that God created them the superior race, and that the rest of us are to serve them.

We know that this does not make sense because we are all descendants of Noah. The Bible states that only Noah's family was saved from the flood that destroyed mankind. Genesis Chapter 8:1 states, "And God remembered Noah, and every living thing, and all the cattle that was with him in the ark: and God made a wind to Passover the earth, and the waters assuaged;" Therefore, we are all one big family, and we all a part of one race of humanity and our brothers and sisters are under a grand delusion.

We must return to the word of God as we are certainly living in the last days. For God to love the world that he gave his only begotten son, so that whosoever believe in him should not perish, but have eternal life. He did not send his son into the world to condemn it, but that the world might be saved through him (John 3:16-17).

In this season of great divide, we must carefully guard our hearts from being polluted with lies, fear, and hatred. We must be the light of the world in this season. It is not time to put our light under a bushel. Mankind needs a savior because the life that we hold onto so dearly is temporary. We are like grass. We are here today, and tomorrow, we will return to the ground. We must remember that most of our existence will be spent in eternity. It is important for us to understand what's going on so that we know how to pray and intercede for the heart of man.

2 Timothy 3:1-5 says, "This know also, that in the last days perilous times shall come. For men shall be lovers of their own selves, covetous, boasters, proud, blasphemers, disobedient to parents, unthankful, unholy, Without natural affection, trucebreakers, false accusers, incontinent, fierce, despisers of those that are good,

Traitors, heady, high minded, lovers of pleasures more than lovers of God; Having a form of godliness but denying the power thereof: *from such turn away."*

Chapter 11
The Rise of Fascism in Western Civilization

The definition of fascism is a political philosophy, movement, or regime (such as that of the Fascist) that exalts nation and often race above the individual and that stands for a centralized autocratic government headed by a dictatorial leader, severe economic and social regimentation, and forcible suppression of opposition. I am not writing to plant fear but so that we can be aware of what is going on in the shadows of this nation. As countries like the United States become more diverse and less white, it creates insecurity and fear.

The number one fear of many white Americans is that the country is being stolen from them through illegal and legal immigration of non-whites who are having more children than they are and who do not embrace the white culture. They are afraid that the culture of whiteness is being destroyed, and they do not like what they are seeing. They feel like society is leaving them behind, and I believe the political leaders are taking advantage of this fear.

In 2016, the year Donald Trump was elected, I had a dream that a spirit of delusion was released in the world that has never been seen before. In the dream, lies were accepted as truth and truth considered lies. In the dream, the number one target of these lies was the next generation because for an ideology to survive and prosper, you must indoctrinate children. I saw great chaos, violence, and protest.

At the end of the dream, I saw what appeared to be normal-looking individuals who were walking the in street and as I looked at their backs, they had wings, and it became clear to me that fallen angels of delusion were released upon the Earth.

We are living in a time of great deception, and deception is creating mistrust in essential institutions in society. This deception preys on the belief that America was better with less diversity and that whites controlled the culture at large. It targets the fear of people who feel like they are losing control and influence on the future of America. One of the most enlightened societies is turning off the light of God and turning on the darkness of conspiracy theories and lies. We have lost our way as a society, and without divine intervention, we are heading to a place of no return.

Pastors who are called to preach the light of Jesus Christ are abandoning the truth for a lie and have bought into conspiracy theories. The church is more politically divided today than ever before. The church is losing the commission given by Jesus Christ to go into the world baptizing and preaching the word of God. We, the church, are losing our saltiness and becoming lukewarm. We have forgotten that Jesus Christ will be returning for his bride. I feel like we are living in a time when the Apostle Paul was writing to the Galatians and asking them, who has bewitched you? Who has caused you to turn from the truth to which you called and to embrace the darkness that we were once ashamed of?

We have more streetlights than ever shining in the streets of the United States, yet it has never been darker. The bible says man loves darkness more than the lights because their deeds are evil. I never thought I would live to see the truth of the bible unfolding right before our eyes at such a rapid pace. As a society, we are willfully turning away from the God that has made this great land prosperous and in turning away from him, we are still expecting to receive all his provisions. As we turn our backs on fundamental truths, we are left with division, increased crime, pestilence, famine, drought, etc. The opposite of prosperity is misfortune, and we are seeing the manifestation of misfortune in this society and the world. We have forgotten that it is he who gives us the power to gain wealth. We have forgotten our first love, and the good news is that He has not forgotten us.

As crime and violence continue to rage in the streets of America, it will not be solved by hiring more law enforcement officers. The heart of man has failed them and has become dark; the only thing that can truly transform the heart of man is the word of God. (2 Chronicles 7:14 King James Version) 14 If my people, which are called by my name, shall humble themselves, and pray, and seek my face, and turn from their wicked ways; then will I hear from heaven, and will forgive their sin, and will heal their land. We need the church to cry out to God for an end-time revival in the streets of the United States of America.

When the world is looking for answers to society's basic problems and when all else has failed, the answer is Jesus Christ. It is time for the churches in America to leave the four walls of their buildings and go into the edges and byways to evangelize the lost and needy. The harvest is reaped, and the need for the light of Jesus is more urgent than ever before.

Coming out of Covid-19 and given the number of people who have lost their lives, there would be a spirit of repentance. I thought we would have a greater need and appreciation for life and the word of God. Covid-19 put us in touch with our mortality and the fact that this world is temporary. This was an opportunity to unite the nation. Instead, it was seen as an opportunity to double down on deception. Moreover, I believe people came out of COVID-19 with less empathy, less kindness, more ruthlessness, and desperation. I thought the churches would be full of people giving their lives to Christ, but it seems emptier.

We have shut Jesus out of almost every institution of government, including schools. It is offensive to talk about the name of Jesus in schools, yet it is okay to talk about witchcraft and other alternative lifestyles. Our children are committing suicide at an alarming rate because we are making them a god unto themselves. As a result, when they come to what they believe is the end of themselves and do not see a way forward, they are prematurely taking their own lives. As America continues to become more paganistic, we are in for tough times.

As a society, we are doing everything possible to remove Jesus. Although he is the reason for the Christmas season, we would rather say "Happy Holidays, Xmas," etc. We do not want Jesus in our personal business because happiness is the truth. We have rejected Jesus and are still expecting God to continue to bless this great nation. We have removed the Son and are still expecting to reap a harvest of love and goodness.

2 Timothy 3:1-17 But know this, that in the last days perilous times will come: For men will be lovers of themselves, lovers of money, boasters, proud, blasphemers, disobedient to parents, unthankful, unholy, unloving, unforgiving, slanderers, without self-control, brutal, despisers of good, traitors, headstrong, haughty, lovers of pleasure rather than lovers of God, having a form of godliness but denying its power. And from such people turn away! For of this sort are those who creep into households and make captives of gullible women loaded down with sins, led away by various lusts, always learning and never able to come to the knowledge of the truth. Now as Jannes and Jambres resisted Moses, so do these also resist the truth: men of corrupt minds, disapproved concerning the faith; but they will progress no further, for their folly will be manifest to all, as theirs also was. But you have carefully followed my doctrine, manner of life, purpose, faith, longsuffering, love, perseverance, persecutions, afflictions, which happened to me at Antioch, at Iconium, at Lystra— what persecutions I endured. And out of them all, the Lord delivered me. Yes, and all who desire to live godly in Christ Jesus will suffer persecution. But evil men and impostors will grow worse and worse, deceiving and being deceived. But you must continue in the things which you have learned and been assured of, knowing from whom you have learned them, and that from childhood you have known the Holy Scriptures, which are able to make you wise for salvation through faith which is in Christ Jesus. All Scripture is given by inspiration of God and is profitable for doctrine, reproof, correction, and instruction in righteousness, that the man of God may be complete, thoroughly equipped for every good work.

America has turned away from the God who made it the beacon of light, even with imperfections, and has turned to political systems to solve its problems. We both understand that man's heart is desperately wicked and is only driven by greed and self-interest.

Many in our society believe that democracy has failed them and would rather have a do-over to regain control. These were some of the sentiments driving those who attacked the capitol on January 6, 2020. They bought into the lies that their votes, which represent their voice, do not matter. Therefore, many Americans were deceived into believing they could not achieve their objective of reshaping America via the political process.

The hope they had in the political process is being destroyed by the lies of their political leaders, and if they cannot trust the governmental institutions, the only way to obtain the desired outcome is through political violence and intimidation. We see today at polling stations that armed masked men are sitting outside in the United States of America, not in Central America, and the Justice System is silent. Fewer white males are graduating college, it is a very dangerous trend, and we should all be concerned.

Luke 21:26-28 - Men's hearts failing them for fear, and for looking after those things which are coming on the earth: for the powers of heaven shall be shaken. And then shall they see the Son of man coming in a cloud with power and great glory. And when these things begin to come to pass, then look up, and lift up your heads; for your redemption draweth nigh.

We are seeing this violence and intimidation all over the nation. Those who are bent toward white supremacy are bolder than ever. They are threatening and committing violence against politicians and school boards if they do not get their way. As this behavior continues to go unchecked by the Justice System, the violent rhetoric and postures are getting out of control. Sadly, I feel like we are living in the 1960s when the Ku Klux Klan reigned supreme, except their target this time around is not just black people, but their own race who do not support their ideologies. The FBI does not monitor domestic white national groups that are recruiting and radicalizing young white males and white military veterans.

As I think of the end-time prophecy about the anti-Christ, there was a time when I could not naturally imagine how a one-world order could happen and that America would not stand for a one-world order. However, given the rise and embrace of conspiracy theories and lies, I am no longer questioning how this could happen. The Bible is the true and infallible word of the living God.

Fascism is on the rise because many people of Western European descent feel they must take matters into their own hands to preserve the lies and ideology that whites are superior. They are willing to walk away from democracy and install a dictator who represents their values and beliefs. This could not happen without the support of the white evangelic base who have surrendered Jesus.

Both political parties have failed the different segments of society. The challenge for many white Americans is that they have always experienced great freedom and prosperity. I am afraid that if we do not correct the course before it's too late, they will remember the good old days and weep with bitter tears.

There will be great mourning and gnashing of teeth if they are awoken to the lies after it's too late. Satan cannot tell the truth; he always deceives us with grandeur, but he never shows us the full picture. I feel that, as a nation, we have entered a covenant with the devil, and we are headed for a great letdown. This puts me in the mind of the prodigal son who had everything he wanted but was not satisfied. It reminds me of Esau, who sold his birthright for a cup of soup; instead, many are selling their birthright for a lie.

In the same way, many people of color have lost hope in the systems of the United States to do the right thing in racial injustice and inequity. Many white Americans are losing hope in society, and a void of hope is despair and violence.

Chapter 12
The Tug of War

I am sure many of us remember the popular game we played in school or at community gatherings: tug of war. It is fair to say that America has entered a period of political tug-of-war, and the two prevailing political ideologies are destroying the nation from within because society has lost sight of Jesus Christ. The political ideologies have divided the nation across all races, genders, religions, and socioeconomic spectrums.

The two enemies of the sustainability of the United States are not ordinary, everyday black and white Americans. The enemies that pose an existential threat to the survivability of this great nation are progressivism and white supremacy. They are both destructive and are leading the nation toward a second civil war. Ordinary Americans are caught up in the power struggle between these two old ideologies and are hating each other for the wrong reasons.

When you speak to everyday white and black Americans, you realize that we both have the same underlying fears and concerns. Our concerns are to live in a country that is free and prosperous, to have the ability to raise our children and provide quality education for them, to live in a society that is free and fair, and to create a better future for our children.

These two political ideologies pull America into two extreme opposite directions while everyday Americans are stuck in the middle and frustrated. Anyone living in America with common sense and discernment can see that the United States is bursting at its seams, and the quality of life has decreased drastically. Basic institutions are falling apart, yet there is no desire to compromise in Washington and fix everyday issues because neither ideologically wants to help the other succeed. There was a time in America when it was country first over politics, and those days are long gone.

We are at a tipping point because every day, Americans, whether you are Christians or non-Christians, black or white we, are being radicalized by these two ideologies.

Yet each ideology speaks of freedom that, at its core, is not true freedom. Freedom of white supremacy is to restrict access to non-white and protect white interests and privileges. As we speak in 2023, states that embrace white supremacy are doing these very things. They are working to restrict voting rights and redraw the political maps because they understand the importance of political representation. If you are a non-white person, you feel like they are trying to take society back to pre-civil rights, and it is terrifying.

Today, once again, white feels empowered to tell you as a black person where and when you don't belong. The days of covert racism are gone. In a society dominated by white supremacy, you will have uprising and instability because society will become unjust and oppressive for non-whites. The solutions to our problems as people of color will be more police officers and more prisons. Those whites may enjoy the good old days, but it is not possible to return to the days when America was great for white Americans because the country is too diverse.

Freedom for the progressive is everything goes, and though you might have more access, society is fair and just. There are no moral standards. Under progressivism, you have moral decay, and though you, as a person of color, may have more access, you are unable to truly enjoy it due to the increase in lawlessness.

I have never seen so much garbage on the streets of America. I have never seen so many broken roads in the United States. I have seen so many people wasting their God-given potential sleeping in tents on the street corners of the richest nation in history. The progressive movement seeks to undo the wrongs of the past but does not address the systematic issues to ultimately make things better at its core. Instead, you have increased government programs that further cripple society and ultimately also turn the haves and the have not against each other.

There was a time when America had genuine Christian values and was considered a Christian nation, but those days were long gone. There was a period in history when America and Europe evangelized the world, but for the first time in history, the United States and Europe needed evangelizing. As America continues to turn its back on God, it has become increasingly lawless and dangerous.

As we as a nation as turned away from God, we have elevated these two ideologies as two religions competing for the soul of the United States. These two anti-Christ ideologies have drawn the battle lines, and for the first time in history, the Unions are in danger of splitting apart. The extremes of the ideologies are so far apart, and their vision for America is so drastically different, and it is becoming more and more difficult to compromise on common sense issues that benefit every American.

Over the past fifty years, the Progressive Movement realized that the key to winning the soul of America was through the education system, and over the past fifty years, the Progressive Movement has successfully removed God from the school and has effectively transformed America via the education system. The education system was successfully used by progressives to slow the mainstream growth of white supremacy and raised a generation of children that subscribed to its ideology.

The battle that we are witnessing in the education system in 2023 is not about what's best for our children and the future of the nation. It is about white supremacy realizing the progressive strategy and looking to take back control of indoctrinating our children and in doing so, reducing the progressive reach and raising a generation of children who believe in white supremacy and its values. We, as ordinary Americans, need to wake up to what's at stake before it is too late and we are pulled into a civil war that will cost countless innocent lives and a country that only exists in our memories.

We must work to strengthen what remains and return to the right standing with our Lord and Savior, Jesus Christ. Like sheep, we have been led away from the only one who can save us and restore the dignity of this nation. We have turned our backs on

God and have believed a lie. We are not learning from third-world nations and why so many of their citizen are flocking to the borders of the United States. When you exalt politics above the country and man above the laws of society, you have violence and corruption. We will all suffer from political violence and corruption. It is time for us to take our heads out of the sand, fall to our knees, and cry out to the God of creation for His mercy and grace for the times that we are living in.

You have increased illiteracy, and the more illiterate the population becomes, the more susceptible to deception and who put all our hope with wicked and brutal men. Whether you are a white or a black person, would you like to live in Russia or Iran? I am sure that the answer would be no, but that is exactly where we are heading if the nation does not change course.

We need a modern-day revival in the streets and the homes of the United States. We need a move of God in the United States. If not, the people will continue to rely increasingly on politicians and corrupt news media to tell them what they want to hear and their version of the truth. In America, we see that conspiracy theories and the doctrine of devils are replacing truth and facts. Therefore, millions of Americans have turned off the truth and tuned into the alter conspiracy theory. This is a problem not just on the right but also on the left. It is becoming increasingly difficult for families to have common sense discussions. Today, you will find families who have fallen victim to these two political ideologies that have divided families and once united communities.

As a result, confidence in basic societal institutions is now at an all-time low. Upholding the rule of law is at an all-time low. The same people who campaigned during the mid-term elections for more law and order to deal with the crimes committed by black people are willing to tear up the rule of law when the law is enforced against those who subscribe to white supremacy.

If you don't believe what I am saying, turn your television channel to Fox and then tune in to CNN or MSNBC, and you will quickly realize that the nation is living in alternate realities that are not sustainable. People have given up on the idea of democracy because they have been deceived. For those who believe in white supremacy, they feel as if democracy has failed them. They feel that society has left them behind and don't see themselves in the progressive ideology. They, too, are terrified, and if things do not change for the better, there will be more white supremacy-motivated political unrest like what was witnessed on January 6th, 2020.

This is why it is foolish to expect gun reforms. The white supremacy sees the progressive as motivated to take away their guns. The strength of white supremacy is their guns. There was a time when they cling to God and guns, but today it is Trump and guns. The strength of the progressive movement is government. These ideologies have infiltrated every aspect of society and government, including the military and the police force, the justice system, and corporate America. When the idea of country first is destroyed, then loyalty is only to the ideology and not the position we serve. This can be witnessed on January 6th, 2020, when law enforcement officers were seen taking pictures with those seeking to overthrow the government.

The progressive ideology has undermined the family by taking rights away from the parent and giving rights to children that they are not mature enough to handle. However, our children are not old enough to apply for credit and student loans with parental assistance. Yet they are old enough to make life-changing decisions, and the schools and doctors are under no obligation to inform the parents because of the child's right to privacy. Our daughter could be pregnant, and the doctor is obligated to let you know what's happening. I believe these are some of the reasons suicides among children are so high in the United States because children are engaging in activities that are detrimental to their souls, and they feel like there is no way out. We are unable to discipline our children, but they are old enough to be killed by the police or to be arrested.

It is fair to argue that the white supremacist movement has tried to colonize the Christian religion and manipulate the word of God to control others. They distort the word of God to fit their agenda and misinformation. The colonization of the word of God, in many ways, created a stumbling block for non-white human beings to relate to the person of Jesus, who is portrayed as someone of European descent. Throughout history, they have misused the word of God and the cross that represents Jesus' ultimate sacrifice for sin for all time. The power of the cross of Christ reconciles humanity with our heavenly Father. In Jesus, we find forgiveness of sin. He was raised from death to give us a new life in Him. In the risen Lord Jesus, we are a new creation.

The white supremacist tried to turn the symbol of the cross into hate and torment. It is such a free thing to discover that the God of the universe is not white, but He is a spiritual being. He can only be spiritually decerned, and He is no respecter of person. In the beginning, He said let us create man in His image. He created one man Adam, and we are all decent of Adam. Who deceives you into thinking that you are superior to other human beings? The portrayed image of God as a white person also feeds the inferiority complex that affects many non-white Americans.

It is such a beautiful thing to see people of all nationalities and colors worshipping and serving the Lord in unity. When we die, we all either go to heaven or hell. There is no special heaven or hell for people of European descent. There is neither Jew nor Gentile, neither slave nor free, nor is there male and female, for you are all one in Christ Jesus. (Galatians 3:28)

On the other hand, the progressive movement sought to remove every evidence of Jesus Christ from society. There was a time when it was correct to say Merry Christmas. They want to enjoy Christmas without acknowledging its true meaning, the birth of Christ. The progressive movement has tried to remove any semblance of the word of God from public places throughout the United States. The name of Jesus is very offensive to the progressive movement, and the bible tells us that they love darkness rather than light because their deeds are evil.

It appears to me that every name is welcome and embraced throughout the progressive movement except the name of Jesus Christ. The progressive movement leaves no evidence for the acts of God because every phenomenon in nature is related to global warming. There is no fear of God anymore because my happiness is the truth. This is one of the reasons there is so much crime and violence in society today because everyone does what is right in their own eyes. Everyone is a law unto themselves.

There was a time when the ideologies found common ground, but now more than ever, they are pulling the country in opposite directions. There is an undercurrent of resentment and hostility that is brewing within the white supremacist movement towards progressives that is very dangerous and concerning. The line is being drawn, and the battle cries are echoing very loudly throughout the white supremacist movement, and it is time for the nation to wake up. They have believed the lies that elections do not work and that they can only win the country back by force. It is time for the people of God to surrender progressivism and white supremacy and put on Jesus Christ.

After World War II, the United States has been the world's police force, the defender of basic freedoms and democracy across the globe. We have spent trillions of dollars on counter-terrorism in the Middle East and all around the world. We have spent trillions of dollars fighting to defeat Al Qaeda and ISIS in the Middle East. How did we turn a hidden eye to the political radicalization of Americans? How did we turn a blind eye to the radicalization of our politicians and institutions in society that are tasked with defending the nation from foreign enemies?

I believe we are being lied to by the media when they make a statement that our democracy is strong. We are one step closer to a political coop than you think. One could argue that the judges throughout the United States and the Supreme Court have been radicalized. The signs are all around. The big threat to the stability of the United States is the political radicalization of its citizens. How did the Justice Department turn a blind eye to Fox News,

AM Radio, and the internet being used as a tool to radicalize its listeners and users to commit political violence?

I know that this book is about the need for healing for African Americans, but we cannot look to this nation to fix our issues and correct all her wrongs when she is bursting at her seams. The United States is not in a healthy place. I believe this is very relevant as to why we need to cry out for a move of God throughout this nation. Pastors with large and small churches have been politically radicalizing, and instead of preaching about the love of Christ and love your enemies, they are using the word of God to radicalize their members.

The preachers are preaching that progressives are demons and are encouraging political violence. They feel as though their country has been stolen from them via the progressive movement, and they will do anything to take it back. This political movement is deeper than anyone can imagine because it is an issue of the heart. The white supremacists believe that this is their fight for survival, and this is their last battle to save the nation. It is time for us to open our eyes and for those of us who are spiritual Christians to fall to our knees and pray for the grace of God to cover this nation.

The ideologies have found their way into the church, and they are diluting the move of God. We are driving the spirit of Christ from the houses of worship because church leaders are embracing and introducing strange doctrines. We are mixing man-made ideologies with the principles of God, and it will not work. We are mixing the doctrine of devils with spiritual truths, and there is a grand dilution sweeping the earth and the churches. The Bible says there will be a great falling away in the last days, and I believe this is happening before our very eyes. We must guard our hearts and itching ears.

The Bible says that we cannot serve two masters; we will love one and hate the other. We have lost our first love and believed a lie. Like a frog being slowly cooked in a pot of water as the temperature is being ever so slightly adjusted, we are losing fervor and faith in Jesus Christ, and the church has become lukewarm. The church has fallen in love with religion and fallen out of love with Jesus Christ.

We have embraced the enemy's schemes because they feel good and easy to follow. We are losing our saltiness, and church doors are closing at an alarming rate throughout the United States. Churches are dying because they are not preaching the good news of Jesus Christ. We have left our first love and are entangled in man-made ideologies. We need the grace of God to stand in this evil day because we have lost sight of good and evil, justice and injustice. As we spend less and less time in the word of God and rely more on pastors and priests for the word of God, we are ripe for deception.

We are being indoctrinated with anti-Christ doctrines at a rapid pace. It is time for us to spiritually come out from among; the bible states that we are in the world, but not of the world. Matthew 7:13-14 states, "Enter through the narrow gate. For wide is the gate and broad is the road that leads to destruction, and many enter through it. But small is the gate and narrow the road that leads to life, and only a few find it."

16 The number of the mounted troops was twice ten thousand times ten thousand. I heard their number. 17 The horses and riders I saw in my vision looked like this: Their breastplates were fiery red, dark blue, and yellow as sulfur. The heads of the horses resembled the heads of lions, and out of their mouths came fire, smoke, and sulfur. 18 A third of mankind was killed by the three plagues of fire, smoke and sulfur that came out of their mouths. 19 The power of the horses was in their mouths and in their tails; for their tails were like snakes, having heads with which they inflict injury. 20 The rest of mankind who were not killed by these plagues still did not repent of the work of their hands; they did not stop worshiping demons, and idols of gold, silver, bronze, stone, and wood—idols that cannot see or hear or walk. 21 Nor did they repent of their murders, their magic arts, their sexual immorality, or their thefts. (Revelation 9:16-21)

You would think that after millions of people lost their lives to COVID-19, there would be a time of repentance throughout the earth. Instead, one could argue that humanity has gotten worse. Our hearts have become more hardened, and our wickedness is at an alarming rate. One trend that I see, which is so beautiful, is that children and young people are surrendering their lives to Jesus Christ. There has been a change in the teachings of pastors who are completely sold out to Jesus Christ. The teachings are grounded in the word of God, and they all confirm each other's sermons through the Holy.

Chapter 13
The Battle for Our Beliefs

2 Thessalonians 2:11-15

For this reason, God sends them a powerful delusion so that they will believe the lie and so that all will be condemned who have not believed the truth but have delighted in wickedness. But we ought always to thank God for you, brothers and sisters loved by the Lord, because God chose you as first fruits to be saved through the sanctifying work of the Spirit and through belief in the truth. He called you to this through our gospel, that you might share in the glory of our Lord Jesus Christ. So then, brothers and sisters, stand firm and hold fast to the teachings we passed on to you, whether by word of mouth or by letter.

There is a battle for what we believe raging throughout the United States that transcends race and religion. It appears to me that we are living in a time where what you believe matters. At the core of the battle for our beliefs is to remove the image of God and replace it with the preservation of self, race, and country. The preservation of race, self, and existence has the potential to affect every Christian if we do not guard our hearts. In its subtlety, it is creeping into our hearts and beliefs, and before you know it, we are loyal to that side.

This is affecting whites and blacks alike. It is affecting the churched and the unchurched. There is a spirit of strong delusion on the earth that is fighting for the hearts and minds of mankind and, at its core, is attacking and eroding our beliefs and fire for God.

The church is more political today than ever before, and we have failed to see that we are not called to be loyal to the Republicans or the Democrats. God has called us to be in the world but not of the world. We are called to be loyal to Christ. Belief has become an idol, and man has exalted his own beliefs above the knowledge of God. A strong delusion and confusion have come over the earth, and we, as believers, are being rocked to sleep. Our devotion and zeal for God have been replaced with our devotion and zeal for politics. We are being indoctrinated and radicalized by the media, except not for the things of Christ but after the fashion of the world.

It is so obvious we are living in the last days because before, I thought it would be so clear to choose the things of God versus the things of the world. Now, with the spirit of delusion and confusion, we are being indoctrinated through what we see and hear, and before knowing, we have drifted so far away from our Savior. It is then you realize the grip and strength of the strongholds that are upon the earth instead of looking for man and our political affiliation to be our savior. The lines are so blurred today that we need the grace of God to remain saved and to open our blinded eyes. So many things are after our hearts, trying to take up residence in our spirits and hearts. Moreover, before you know it, our allegiance to the things of Christ is divided.

In 2008, when President Obama was elected, a spirit of delusion came over the black evangelic Christians; it entered our hearts and blinded our eyes to the abomination spirit that was later released into the earth. This was done under the disguise of the first black president elected in the United States of America and the pride and excitement given our history of hardship and struggle in the United States. He represented hope and a can-do spirit. His election removed limitations on what we can accomplish and reminded us that the American dream is still attainable. This allowed him and politicians to enter our hearts. Moreover, his grip on our heartstrings blinded our eyes when the spirit of abomination was released in the United States and the world.

Today, black evangelic Christians are more politically inclined than ever before, and our devotion to politics is now competing with our devotion to God. The enemy of our soul always comes in unassuming and before we know it, we have lost our spirit of being objective and have become loyal followers. The black evangelic is under attack and the struggle is to shake off the grip, stronghold, and delusion that came over the church when President Obama became elected.

Many of us, before President Obama, strongly did not believe in abortion but have become comfortable with the idea of abortion. There are many things that we rejected and would not tolerate before President Obama that we have become comfortable with. We are under a spirit of grand delusion, and this is competing with our devotion to Christ and the word of God. Before President Obama, one could argue that we were more conservative in our beliefs of God. It was easier for us to see right from wrong. We surely did not embrace the spirit of abomination that is sweeping through the earth. It was easier for us to choose God over politics. It is important for us to participate in the political process, but not at the expense of our core beliefs in God.

Before President Obama was elected, a United States president had to show that they have embraced core Christian beliefs. Even if it was not genuine, there was a break to the Christian values and beliefs. This seems to have been an unspoken expectation of everyone who wanted to serve as a President and win the Christian vote. Since President Obama in his second term invoked the spirit of abomination, this standard has been removed.

Likewise, when Donald Trump ran for president and became elected, a strong spirit of deception and delusion came over the white evangelicals and today, many white evangelicals seem to be more loyal to country and politics than they are to God. Many White Americans have given up their beliefs in God and have embraced Qanun. It has become so hard for the people of God to discern truth from lies. They have given up their belief in Christ and have elevated Donald Trump as God. The same effect Barrack Obama had on black evangelicals; Donald Trump is having the same effect on white evangelic Christians. The end results are the church is being radicalized, but not after the things of God. We have turned away from the truth and our calling and embraced darkness.

My conclusion is that neither political party is good for the people of God. They have both been radicalized and have both embraced extremisms as their core beliefs. Both parties are promoting extremisms. The Republican party promotes white supremacy and the intolerance of others and the unwavering devotion to guns. The Democratic party is promoting extremisms in the areas of self-hatred, abortion, drug abuse, and moral decline. Both parties have embraced the decline in authority and rules of law that do not only apply to certain races. The rules of law have been misused and abused by both parties for political gain.

Both parties are dealing with a spirit of confusion and delusion. In the Democratic party, it is manifested in gender confusion. In the Republican party, this is manifested as delusions that white humanity is superior to other humans who have also been created in the likeness and image of God. Both parties have embraced misinformation and lies. It is becoming more and more difficult to be an independent thinker.

Extremisms in the Republic party is intolerant by the mainstream media because it is the evil we know throughout the history of the United States. On the other hand, extremisms in the Democratic party are more tolerated, because of how it is packaged. It is packaged as considerably more freedoms, but in turn, it is perpetuating more spiritual bondages. Romance 6: 16 16 Don't you know that when you offer yourselves to someone as obedient slaves, you are slaves of the one you obey— whether you are slaves to sin, which leads to death, or obedience, which leads to righteousness? In the end, both will destroy of the United States of America. Extremism in the Democratic party hates the image of God and His followers. Both parties are invoking a spirit of poverty and desolation in the soul of mankind and society.

Since the United States has turned away from God and embraced man's wisdom, we have lacked the spirit of moderation.

We are sinking deeper and deeper into a state of no return because both extremes within politics have their own core beliefs of what America should look like, and there is no middle ground and hardly any room for compromise. There is a way that seems right to a man, but the end is the way of destruction. Proverbs 14:10. Each party is trying very hard to shape the United States in their own image, and we are moving further from the image of God at the core of this nation.

Therefore, going forward, we will consistently tire down the previous administration's accomplishments and start over depending on which party is in power. It is not what's best for the United States of America anymore; it is what's best for the party and their guiding principles. This mindset is pulling us closer and closer to political violence. This is taking a toll on families who have become divided based on which party they vote for. In a sense, we have become a divided third-world nation, which is why there is so much instability and poverty in the third nations. As men in this nation become less and less educated, they stop reasoning with their intelligence but with their hearts and ignorance. America has fallen from the beacon on the hill because we have lost sight of what's most important and have decided to worship money, self-preservation, politics, country, and materialism.

I pray that a spirit of repentance will come upon the earth, beginning in the house of God. It is becoming more difficult to say that we are Christian without offending others. It has become offensive in the United States to mention the name of Jesus. The name of Jesus is being erased from every facet of society. We are comfortable with witchcraft and other religions, but the name of Jesus conflicts with sin and causes offense. Therefore, it is offensive and is being redefined as the root of hate speech. The day is coming when Christianity will be seen as an extremist religion.

Chapter 14
We Are Overcomers

I beseech you therefore, brethren, by the mercies of God, that ye present your bodies a living sacrifice, holy, acceptable unto God, which is your reasonable service. And be not conformed to this world: but be ye transformed by the renewing of your mind, that ye may prove what is that good, and acceptable, and perfect, will of God. (Romans 12:1-2)

I the Lord have called thee in righteousness, and will hold thine hand, and will keep thee, and give thee for a covenant of the people, for a light of the Gentiles; to open the blind eyes, to bring out the prisoners from the prison, and them that sit in darkness out of the prison house (Isaiah 42:6-7).

How can we be set free from the scars of slavery when we never physically experienced it? We must embrace our past, that our ancestors were slaves. However, slavery does not define us as a people. The journey of our people in America tells an underlying truth about who we are as a people. We are created strong by our creator. Despite the inhumane hardships we endured for over four hundred years and are still enduring. God allowed us to persevere. When there were plans implemented to institutionalize us and permanently make us slaves mentally. God already had a plan to heal and deliver us to take on His image and likeness.

His word says that He will not allow us "to be tested more than what we are able to endure." Instead of dwelling on what we were, let's learn from the past and focus on who we are and who we are. We are the redeemed. We are the set apart. We are God's workmanship created in Christ Jesus for good works. We were not destined to fail. Instead, we were destined to triumph over physical and mental slavery so that we might give God glory and honor through Jesus Christ.

How do we begin to set free a mind that has been sealed tight by the abuse and trauma of our ancestors without instructions on how to open it without destroying the fabric of its being? Slavery was not only a physical reality, but slavery was also a state of mind. We are still struggling with the mindset of a slave. The mindset we do not matter, and our race is inferior to the white race. The mindset of hopelessness. The mindset that we need to be rescued by politicians.

Moreover, the evidence says otherwise. I believe no other race could have endured what we went through and not be consumed. The mindset of a slave causes you to die for your own purpose and humanity. Resocialization strips you of your identity and from having a sense of purpose. You take on the purpose and identity of your master. You take pride in your master and strive to undermine those who looks like you. Especially if they are thinking independently and experiencing success. We are still struggling with the mindset of a servant. We were institutionalized in our thinking so that we would not be able to survive without depending on the system or our "master" for the instruction on how to function.

I believe the goal of "institutionalized thinking" was the reasoning behind building so many prisons as opposed to an emphasis on building schools and focusing on integration. It was evident that with the goal of institutionalization, many of our people would not be able to survive outside of what was established for slaves. This was the primary reason we were denied the right to be enlightened through education. The goal of "institutionalized thinking" was meant to be irreversible. We were destined to live as babysitters, handymen, and helpers. Our sole purpose would be to maintain our master's way of life.

If you successfully keep someone in absolute darkness in their minds, then they will always be the servants of those that have their minds enlightened. The system of America expected our people to fail. The system of America was designed for those to prosper who have been enlightened through intellect. This "enlightenment" is necessary to prosper and successfully navigate the American system.

Being denied the right to read and learn was crucial to maintaining the "slave mentality" and keeping us in darkness. Still, to this day, because of the darkness of our minds, we don't fully understand the importance of having an education. Often our children are still being provided with inadequate education and substandard deliberately.

The education they are receiving is just enough to barely survive and maintain a marginal lifestyle. The education most of our children receive is non-competitive, and with it, no one is in danger of becoming successful. Even though the laws no longer deny us the right to be educated, we are still wrestling against the mindset of our ancestors. For many of us, it still stands true the best place to hide something from a black person is in a book. Our minds need to be set free from the bondage of a slave mindset.

How can the base of our minds be penetrated so that new life can begin to take place? When we give our lives to Jesus, His words begin to reprogram our minds to see ourselves the way He sees us, not as a descendent of slaves, but His creation. We are a life that was worth sending His only begotten son to die for. In His word, he said, "Let us make man in our image." God created us to prosper. He created us to have dominion over the earth. He created us to subdue the earth. He created us to replenish the earth, and most of all, He created us to worship Him. Would God die and require us, an inferior people, to worship Him? If He knows the little insignificant sparrows that fly by the air, how much more will He know and love you, who he created to worship Him and spend eternity with Him?

How do we begin to cut away the hopelessness, inferiority, poor self-esteem, and inadequacy from the base of our minds and souls so that light can begin to shine in and bring about the needed healing? We must stop believing the lies that Christianity is a white man's religion and embrace the fact that Jesus is spirit; therefore, we must worship him in spirit and in truth. In the same way, the things of God enlighten us and teaches us how to operate in the spirit. So, does education teach us how to flourish in the economic system created by man? The truth about Jesus is in His word. For God so love the (you and me) world that he gave his only begotten son that whosoever believes in him should not perish but have everlasting life.

In Jesus, there is a light of life. There is a light of hope. There is a light of change. There is a light of a new beginning. There is light of a new season. There is a light of love. There is a light of acceptance. There is a light that shows we are competent. There is a light that shows we have more than enough within us to succeed.

The light that we are is a gift created and purposed by the love of God. There is a light that is being shown to us that we have a Savior who felt and bore our heavy cross. A light is leading us on a journey closer to the Savior, who hears and empathizes with our cries when we feel mistreated and oppressed. There is a light of redemption being offered to each one of us, no matter who we are or where we were born. A light of reconciliation is offered through the shed blood of the Savior. A light of new birth will deliver us from our old curse.

Then spake Jesus again unto them, saying, I am the light of the world: he that followeth me shall not walk in darkness, but shall have the light of life. (John 8:12)

Jesus said, He is the light of the world. He also said if He sets you free then you are truly free indeed. We have a High Priest who can relate to our broken heartedness. (Hebrews 4:14-15) He can put our minds and emotions back together to experience the joy of His light. He came to set the captives free and release the prisoners of war.

How do we begin to connect the pieces that bridge the past, the present, and the future so a new season can begin? We need a Savior for our minds. He is a Savior who understands. He is a Savior who has been bound. He is a Savior who has been beaten. He is a Savior who has been scorned. He is a Savior who was forsaken. He is a Savior who had no place to lay His head. He is a Savior who was locked up and chained.

He is a Savior who died and went down into the pit of hell and now has the key to life that can release us from the bondage of hell and even the grave. He is a Savior who can reach deep down into the depths of our souls and remove the overhanging bushes of our minds so that the power of light and life can begin to shine not only in us but through us. We can have hope in a new beginning through this Savior!

Freedom a Call to Healing

Chapter 15
Arise

See, I am doing a new thing! Now it springs up; do you not perceive it? The wild animals honor me, the jackals, and the I am making a way in the wilderness and streams in the wasteland. The wild animals honor me, the jackals and the owls, because I provide water in the wilderness and streams in the wasteland, to give drink to my people, my chosen, the people I formed for myself that they may proclaim my praise. (Isaiah 43:19–21)

Despite the decks stacked against us, we continue to rise and seize the opportunities before us. We must embrace our creativity, the need for education, entrepreneurship, women empowerment, and mentorship. About four years ago, I attended a women's empowerment conference, and I was astonished at what the collective effort of women can achieve when working together. They brought successful women from all different backgrounds to share their stories of how they made it and the challenges they faced along the way. As I was sitting in the conference, it dawned on me that the black women are being empowered to over the limitation of their ability to achieve.

They uplifted each other through role models of other successful women who saw it necessary to give back. Their chains and the scales over their eyes were being chattered so that they could see what was in front of them and know that they had the support system to achieve whatever they set their mind to accomplish. The mental ceiling of how far they can climb was being destroyed. I asked myself at that moment, what about black men? Who is empowering them to overcome their limitations and see that there is a world that is bigger than where they live? Who is telling them that they have a choice? I left the conference feeling excited for the women but depressed about the state of black men.

It is time for us to arise and take control of our need for mental and spiritual healing. We have spent centuries fighting for our physical freedom. It is time for us to look inward and cry out to God for the healing of our minds. We will never be truly free as a people until we break the shackles from our minds and discover our true worth. It is time to shake off underachievement and embrace the fact that we have God-given purpose. We can achieve whatever we set our minds to accomplish with hard work, consistency, commitment and perseverance. We must become our brother's and sister's keepers. Each one help one and look to each other and God for what we need. Even though many of us as people have overcome and are doing well, we have a large segment that is not doing so well.

Therefore, it requires us to give back to help those still stuck in the cycle that committing crime is the only option available to gain success. Our young people need to know that they will live into their older years and that they can choose between a life of violence and go on to achieving their dreams. Although weapons are formed against us, they will not win. The dangerous thing about the mind is that once you learn what is necessary to stay alive in an oppressed situation, you begin to teach the next generation the exact behaviors. Before you know it, generations have passed, and those things become almost hereditary. You can be physically free, but mentally you are still in chains.

Can you imagine the fearful habits and behaviors passed down from our ancestors?

Our soul needs spiritual fire to burn away the limitations, fears, incapacitations, and inferior complexes that cloud our minds, but the blood of Jesus is hot enough and strong enough to burn the scars from our minds. The blood of Jesus can flow within the canvas of our minds and begin to set free the gifts sealed within us. Then, a new season will dawn, and those who were once prisoners of war can live to sing a new song.

Behold, the former things are come to pass, and a new thing do I declare before they spring forth, I tell you of them. Sing unto the

Lord a new song and his praise from the end of the earth. (Isaiah 42:1)

We will sing a song of love. We will sing a song of true and complete freedom. We will sing a song that we are free to live, free to feel, free to give, and free to receive. We are free to move forward, no longer caught in a stream as a leaf settling between two stones. We are no longer tossed to and fro by the forces of the environment around us, with no power to change course.

We are free to choose and free to just be. We are free to embrace the journey God has crafted for us. We are free from the chains in our minds and free from the shame of our past. We are free to take our place in society with no more limitations set forth by the ghost of war. We are no longer prisoners of war but a people with a purpose. We are a people who bring hope to others through Christ, who has come to set all the captives free.

I alone know the plans I have for you, plans to bring you prosperity and not disaster, plans to bring about the future you hope for (Jeremiah 29:11).

The Will to Overcome

We are a people destined to live and connect to who we were created to be. We were fashioned and created in the image of God our Father. We are a people fully restored. When we are healed and delivered, we will realize that the war is over and that peace is at hand. We can begin to pick up the pieces of our lives and connect to where we are now and where God has destined us to go.

We are people who can change where we are. We are a people who can go far and are not dependent on the government for handouts. We are a people fully capable of answering life's call. We are a people who are no longer stuck but a mighty army ready to invade. We will take back what was stolen and restore that which was lost.

You are part of this as well. Your chains can be broken as you come to the foot of the cross, where Jesus shed His blood for your sins. Receive the inheritance given to you through Jesus Christ. Claim your authority and cry out to your God for help. Do not accept the lies of the devil spoken into your life, whether through a teacher, a friend, someone in authority or a parent. Resist the devil and he will flee from you. All you need to do is draw near to God and He will draw near to you.

Accept the Lord's calling on your life and enter a lifetime of healing and deliverance. You are His workmanship. You are His heart's desire. He feels your pain and hurt. He hears your every cry. You are never alone. He is always there waiting for you to invite Him into your situation. He will not override your free will, so you must call out to Him.

You must recognize your need and dependence on Him. You must receive and embrace Him as your Heavenly Father. You must surrender your will and desire to Him. He is your Father, and His thoughts toward you are for good. His plan and purpose for your life are perfect.

Chapter 16
A Call to Deal with the Past

The past is not always easy to confront, but to move forward and embrace our present, we must acknowledge our past. We must be willing to accept it even though it is painful, shameful, and may leave us in a place of vulnerability. Remember, the broken and contrite heart, He will not despise.

Throughout the Old and New Testament, one of the primary warnings from the Lord is that if we hear His voice, we should not harden our hearts. One way we harden our hearts is by not being able to receive the healing available from our past. As a result, the word of God becomes null and void because we do not apply faith to His promises for our lives.

God often uses unusual methods to get His message to us. We need to be alert to His call and not miss out on the opportunity to receive from Him. When Moses saw the burning bush, it did not make any sense in his natural mind. Moses chose to believe God despite his feelings and thoughts at the time. Moses did not deny his struggles. He was very open and honest with the Lord about his insecurities and poor self-image. As a result of Moses' honesty and heart to please God, he was propelled into his ministry. Moses could have felt he was unjustly treated, and the circumstances of his past could have kept him trapped in emotional bondage. Instead, he faced his past, acknowledged it happened, and allowed God to use him to not only save himself, but an entire nation.

At some point it is necessary to realize that we must embrace our past in a positive and direct way. It must not be in the spirit of blaming those we believe are the cause of our suffering, but of acknowledging it happened so we can move forward and save ourselves and our young people. God is willing and able to heal us, but we must cry out to Him from our hearts as did the children of Israel and He will be hastened to respond.

Do not harden your heart. I believe Jesus is inviting the black community to come and dine at His feast, where everything we need to be made whole is at His table. God's grace is free to everyone who is willing to accept His invitation. It is not by works; it is by faith. The season of healing for the black community is at hand. Jesus of Nazareth is calling us to attend His great feast.

Cry out to Him while He is near. He has a plan and purpose for our lives. It is time to return to Jesus Christ, the author and finisher of our faith. Allow Jesus to search our hearts and heal the areas where we need our own specific healing. Use this Psalm as your prayer today.

O LORD, you have searched me, and you know me. You know when I sit and when I rise; you perceive my thoughts from afar. You discern my going out and my lying down; you are familiar with all my ways. Before a word is on my tongue you know it completely, O LORD. You hem me in--behind and before; you have laid your hand upon me. Such knowledge is too wonderful for me, too lofty for me to attain.

Where can I go from your Spirit? Where can I flee from your presence? If I go up to the heavens, you are there; if I make my bed in the depths, you are there. If I rise on the wings of the dawn, if I settle on the far side of the sea, even there your hand will guide me, your right hand will hold me fast. If I say, "Surely the darkness will hide me and the light become night around me," even the darkness will not be dark to you; the night will shine like the day, for darkness is as light to you.

For you created my inmost being you knit me together in my mother's womb. I praise you because I am fearfully and wonderfully made; your works are wonderful; I know that full well. My frame was not hidden from you when I was made in the secret place. When I was woven together in the depths of the earth, your eyes saw my unformed body. All the days ordained for me were written in your book before one of them came to be. How precious to me are your thoughts, O God! How vast is the sum of them! Was I to count them; they would outnumber the grains of sand? When I awake, I am still with you. If only you would slay the wicked, O God!

Away from me, you bloodthirsty men! They speak of you with evil intent; your adversaries misuse your name. Do I not hate those who hate you, O LORD, and abhor those who revolt against you? I have nothing but hatred for them; I count them my enemies. Search me, O God, and know my heart; test me and know my anxious thoughts. See if there is any offensive way in me and lead me in the way everlasting. (Psalm 139)

Freedom a Call to Healing

Chapter 17
A Call to Healing

Our souls need the blood of Jesus to burn away the entanglements and bondage of our minds. When this occurs, the light of Jesus can begin to shine deep down into the depths of our being. Plants need the light of the sun to grow and produce fruit. Likewise, our souls need the light of Jesus to illuminate our minds. It is then that deep and lasting healing can begin to take place. Jesus wants to restore our broken hearts, emotions, and spirits. He wants to bring us back to Himself and His word.

Jesus wants to pour the Holy Spirit into the depth of our being to begin a process of true and lasting restoration of our body, soul, and spirit. He wants to build a new wineskin within our spirit. He wants to transform and renew our minds so that we can fully understand and declare that old things have passed away, and behold, all things have become new. (2 Corinthians 5:17)

A new wine is a renewed mind and heart. Sometimes the process of true and lasting healing comes to us through an invitation. The invitation from the Lord does not require us to fix it and make it right. Come in your brokenness. Come with your mess. Come with your chains. Come if you are on drugs. Come if you are homeless and hopeless. Come if you are a prostitute. Come if you are a drug dealer. Therefore, we must choose whether to stay in our current place of safety or be willing to risk it all and step forward to accept the invitation, take up our cross, and follow Him daily.

Healing often requires a response from us. That response can either move us closer to our deliverance or push us further back due to unbelief. Even in today's world, Jesus is still in the business of healing and deliverance.

The Invitation

An invitation for healing only requires your acceptance that you are not able to do it through mind power or mental manipulation but that it is a process. You need to accept an intervention of healing and deliverance that Jesus Christ can give you, and sometimes, He will allow your healing to come through counseling.

The acceptance of the invitation for healing requires a measure of faith. The measure of faith sometimes depends on our awareness of our need, which comes through a doctor's visit, the loss of a loved one or a deep anguish groaning in our soul.

The last resort, which leads to desperation, is when we have nowhere else to turn, have tried everything known to man, and are finally at our wits' end. This is the way many of us finally accept God's intervention.

How badly do we want to receive our healing?

Do we believe that we will be healed even if all we do is touch Jesus' garment?

The woman with the issue of blood was at her wits' end. She had tried every remedy known to man, and her problem was not answered. One day, she saw Jesus and was willing to risk it all for the opportunity to finally experience the freedom and completeness she so long desired. She pushed through until she could touch the hem of His garment. When she did, Jesus told her that it was because of her faith that she was healed. (Matthew 9:20-22)

Another example is the lame man who had been sitting for thirty- eight years waiting for the water to be troubled so he could receive his healing. Each time the water was troubled he could not make it into the water on time. Therefore, when Jesus came and offered an invitation for his healing, he did not want to miss it. He was willing to do what Jesus told him, though it did not make sense to him at the time. (John 5:1-16)

Are we waiting for someone else to exercise their faith on our behalf?

Are we willing participants in our healing process?

A Call to Healing

What if no one is there to pick us up and bring us to the water when it is troubled?

Are we willing to lose our current safe place to receive our healing?

Are we going to continue waiting for the perfect opportunity for healing that requires no sacrifice or acceptance?

In the New Testament, almost every time Jesus performed a healing, He required something of the person being healed. The blind man cried to Jesus for help and persisted even when others told him to be quiet. Then Jesus did not heal him in his current position. Jesus asked him to come out of his place of comfort. He instructed the blind man to go to the pool and wash his face. If they were lame, he required them to stand up and take those first steps toward healing. Each time, Jesus challenged the individual to activate their faith.

Imagine if you are a lame person and someone tells you that you are healed and instructs you to exercise your faith and stand up without assistance. Would you believe? What if Jesus instructed you to take up your bed and walk? Would you interrupt His offer for healing and tell Him you are lame and cannot stand? Do you know Jesus is aware of your current state and infirmity?

Many would ask why we pray for healing. Whenever you ask for healing, you activate your faith, which will keep you in a state of healing. One of the first steps in healing is the awareness that you need healing. Once you are healed, it needs to become your testimony to others. Healing provokes an outward declaration.

[Call out] When you are healed, you are not just healed for yourself. You are healed for someone else who is still going through exactly what you were delivered from.

Someone needs to hear your testimony so they, too, can believe and be set free. When you confess your healing, faith is infused in the person seeking healing. When God delivers and heals you, you are not to be ashamed of your deliverance. You are not to be afraid to embrace where God has now placed you. Embrace your healing, knowing God is in control of your situation.

Freedom a Call to Healing

Chapter 18
A Call to Forgiveness

For if we forgive men their trespasses, your heavenly father will also forgive you: but if ye forgive not men their trespasses, neither will your father forgive your trespasses. (Matthew 6:14-15)

We are no longer victims. Instead, we are a people who can achieve and forgive. Instead of seeking revenge for what He had to endure, Jesus said, "Father, forgive them; for they know not what they do" (Luke 23:34). Jesus knew that freedom comes through true forgiveness of those who have wronged you. Sometimes, it is especially hard to forgive those who have taken something very valuable from you, like those who have tried to destroy your sense of worth, your sense of purpose, and your identity, quite frankly, who are still trying to use the same tactics of old.

As hard as it can be to forgive those who constantly seek to oppress us, the forgiveness is for us, not for them. The forgiveness is for you. The best way to defeat an enemy is through forgiveness because they no longer have the power to control you. If you take power back through forgiveness, they cannot use your emotions against you. The power to trigger our emotional response will subside, and instead, we can engage them in a conversation to help them see their bigotry that sometimes they are not even aware. Racism is a culture and an American value. Currently, it is seen daily all over social media that white people are trying to trigger the black emotional response via insult and harassment. It is up to us to pick up the pieces of our lives and stop giving them an excuse to use the power of the enforcement against us.

Forgiveness requires us to confess our pain and stop hiding it inside. The Bible says, "Confess your faults one to another" (James 5:16). This can be done in families. Get together and talk about the pain and scars of the American experience. Tell this generation how we held it together, how we overcame it, and that we are still struggling. Chances are they are struggling with the same things but dealing with it in a different way.

Moreover, forgiveness is a key to reconciliation. Forgiveness is not only the prerequisite for being reconciled to God; it also allows us to be reconciled to each other and ourselves. In every instance, you cannot have a genuine and lasting relationship without forgiveness.

For example, my mother immigrated to the United States when I was three years old. At the age of seventeen, I was reunited with my mother, but another seventeen years went by before I could have a close relationship with her. Our relationship was always shallow. I did not realize that the underlying issue I was dealing with was unforgiveness. My ability to forgive her freed me and gave me the permission to move forward to the next stages of my growth.

Sometimes, the process of forgiveness requires another party, which could be a therapist or a pastor. When we entertain unforgiveness, it is a sin against God. Can we really count the number of times we have sinned against him? Because of His great love towards us He does not hold it to our account? The sin of unforgiveness turns into a dark cloud that blocks out the light of God from shining into our lives. That is why we feel hopeless and convince ourselves we will spend the rest of our lives in darkness and despair.

The moment we confess our sins, the process of death stops. The darkness that hovers over us like a dark cloud is removed, and the light of God can now begin to shine into our lives. The disconnection we feel from the Lord because of sin is removed when we confess, let go of guilt and shame, and trust the Lord. He forgives us irrespective of our sins, and we are reconciled back to Him.

The number one thing that keeps us from confessing that we need help with mental illness and receiving our deliverance is pride and the of being stigmatized. Pride says we do not need help. We are ashamed to cry out, fearing what others might say. We do not want to appear weak or vulnerable because we want others to perceive us as strong and have our lives together.

To experience deliverance through confession, you must be humble and unashamed. For example, the man in the Bible who was sick and his friends heard about the healing power of Jesus. They brought him to Jesus, but the room was full, and there was no way for them to enter the building where Jesus was sitting. Determined to get their friend to Jesus, they cut a hole in the ceiling and let their friend down right in front of Jesus. Astonished by the men's faith, Jesus told the sick man his sins were forgiven and to take up his bed and walk. For this man to receive his miracle, he had to be willing to walk out his faith. The man showed a humble spirit when he immediately followed Jesus' instructions without worrying about what others would think of him. (see Mark 2:1-12)

A Gentile woman heard about Jesus and came to Him for her young daughter who had an unclean spirit. She came and humbly fell at His feet. She kept asking Him to cast the demon out of her daughter.

Jesus said to her, "Let the children be filled first, for it is not good to take the children's bread and throw it to the little dogs." And she answered and said to Him, "Yes, Lord, yet even the little dogs under the table eat from the children's crumbs." Then He told her, "For these sayings go your way; the demon has gone out of your daughter." And when she had come to her house, she found the demon gone out and her daughter lying on the bed. (Mark 7:25-30; see also Matthew 15:21-28)

She is often cited for great faith, but I believe her humility propelled her into great faith.

Chapter 19
The Gift of Forgiveness

"Therefore, if any man be in Christ, he is a new creature: old things are passed away; behold, all things are become new." 2 Corinthians 5:17

I believe 2 Corinthians 5:17 perfectly demonstrates God's redemptive plan. When we surrender our lives to Him, He wipes the slate clean. Old things have passed away. Everything sins we committed before receiving the gift of salvation, He has cast them into the sea of forgetfulness, and he remembers them no more. Though we remember them and may still feel guilt and shame, he has wiped our slate clean and given us a new beginning in Himself. From that moment onward, when He looks at you, he sees the image of His son who suffered, died, and rose again on the third day to reconcile us back to Himself.

Over the course of my life, I have realized that forgiveness is a gift, and it gives us the grace to start over anew. Forgiveness is a choice. The road to forgiveness can be long and painful because it often leaves us vulnerable, especially if the other individual does not validate our hurt and acknowledge their wrongdoing. In those instances, the tendency is to withdraw and withhold our forgiveness.

Forgiveness can be instant, but sometimes forgiveness is a process. However, we must remember that forgiveness is a gift from God that frees the human soul. The foundation of our relationship with God is based on forgiveness. He forgave us for our transgressions against him. Without forgiveness, there is no remission of sin. Without forgiveness, there is no right standing with God. When we make the decision to forgive, we are pruning our souls and cutting away those feelings and emotions in us that don't bear fruit. We are cutting away the heavy burdens that weigh us down. Forgiveness is like a fire burning through the forest, and after the rain, you have a new life. Forgiveness is the door to reconciliation.

Forgiveness can feel like you are letting the other person off the hook. Sometimes, we may feel like the person is not worthy of our forgiveness and are justified in our feelings. Moreover, forgiveness is for you, not them; it is for you. They may have moved on while you are still stuck, they may not have placed the same value on your pain, and they have no idea how you feel. They have a completely different perspective and wonder what is wrong with you. Start by asking the Lord to help you forgive yourself, especially if you hold yourself responsible for the outcome of the situation.

The Lord says if we don't forgive others, we will not be forgiven for our sins. We have the ultimate judge who will judge every man for their choices, and that person is Jesus. Oftentimes, forgiveness has many layers. It does not mean you must have a relationship with someone because you forgive someone. You must surrender the person or situation to the Lord and get out of the way for him to do a work on the individual. When you forgive, you relinquish control, and the healing process can begin.

Unforgiveness is like an abscess; forgiveness is cutting the abscess to release impurities. Without forgiveness, the wound can never be healed, and you are free to move forward. You are a slave to the person you refuse to forgive. When I emigrated to the United States at the age of 17, my stepfather took me to see my father before leaving Jamaica to live in the United States, and the only words he uttered to me were to be respectful to my stepfather. For many years after, I was heartbroken that my father did not love me as a son. I felt unwanted.

For the next ten years, I had no communication with my father. Over the ten-year period, the Lord started showing me my anger and resentment towards my father. Due to the fact we had no relationship there was no opportunity to resolve my feelings towards him. Until one night, I was watching a Dr. Charles Stanley Sermon about forgiveness. At the end of the sermon, he offered an invitation to forgive my parents or anyone who had scarred me. He stated whether the person is alive or dead, I must forgive to set myself free and move forward. It was that night I made the decision to forgive my father.

Dr. Stanley instructed the listeners to set aside a chair and pretend the person was sitting on it. Then, the person told them everything they had ever done to them and, in the end, offered them forgiveness. I remember feeling a release at the end of the exercise. In the moments afterward, I felt no more anger and resentment toward my father.

In 2017, when my grandmother passed. I went to her funeral in Jamaica. I was now 34 years old and had the opportunity to see my father again; as much as I wanted to have the long-awaited conversation with him after a brief interaction. I concluded that he wasn't in the position as an individual to receive or acknowledge my hurt. At that moment, I realized that to move forward with my life, I must be willing to acknowledge that what I wanted from my father as a son he was not able to offer to give of himself since he didn't have to offer it to himself.

Those who cause us tremendous pain are sometimes blinded by their guilt, denial, and wounds. Therefore, they lack compassion and empathy and are unable to acknowledge our hurt. I accepted the situation for what it was now. I felt compassion for him because, for the first time, I saw my father as a man who was also broken and lost.

I turned it over to the Lord because I accepted that the issue was bigger than my father and me. It was a generational issue plaguing the family lineage. Five years later, I received a message from my father asking me why I had isolated myself from him, and that opened the door for us to have a grown-up conversation. Since I had forgiven him and had no expectation of him, it allowed us to work on our relationship.

The Grace to Forgive Ourselves

When we think of forgiveness, we often think about receiving or extending forgiveness to others. It is just as important to forgive oneself. Parents often find it very difficult to forgive themselves when they make decisions that intentionally or unintentionally harm their children. The worst example of struggling to forgive oneself is unresolved issues with a loved one who passes away.

We often struggle to forgive ourselves when we are engaging in secret sin or inequity. If you are the victim of sexual harassment, molestation, or rape, the tendency is to blame yourself, and you often feel unclean. If you have an abortion due to an unplanned pregnancy, many women struggle to forgive themselves. Whatever the situation, sometimes we find it easier to forgive while withholding forgiveness from ourselves.

Unforgiveness towards others often manifests in how we treat them. Unforgiveness towards oneself is often hidden and can manifest itself in depression, alcoholism, drug abuse, suicide, etc. We mentally and emotionally abuse ourselves and fill our lives with business and stuff. We try very hard to avoid being alone with ourselves, and we fill our lives with business. The Lord wants us to confront our issues and see his grace in our pain.

We can accept the Lord Jesus into our lives and set others free from their bondage. While we still don't believe we are worthy of forgiveness and suffer in silence. Knowing that you would mess up before the foundation of the world, our Abba Father still sends Jesus Christ into the world to die on the cross to redeem you from all your mishaps. Will you receive His forgiveness today? Will you take him at His word and forgive yourself? John 3:16-17 states that Jesus died to set the captive free, and that covers forgiving yourself. Perfect love covers a multitude of sins. We must receive his forgiveness to be free in our relationship with the Lord.

Chapter 20
Stages of Deliverance

God's Revelation to Me in a Dream. In my dream, the Lord revealed to me that there are four stages of deliverance:

- Having no hope.
- Craving deliverance.
- Being set free.
- The fight to remain free.

The first stage is the very dark stage, where there appears to be no hope or escape from your bondage. In this stage, you are in absolute darkness, and there appears to be no end to your current struggle. This is the stage where many people decide to give up on life and commit suicide. It feels like you will spend the rest of your life stuck, and there is no way you can be delivered from your hopelessness.

The Lord also showed me that in the first stage, you begin to see light shining ahead of you, leading you toward the second stage, and you begin to crave deliverance. The light you are seeing as you enter the second stage is a glimmer of hope. However, when you are delivered from the first stage of your bondage, you think you are free, only to realize that even though you are functioning better, you are still stuck. In stage two, you begin to have more hope. In this stage, you begin to seek deliverance, but you still cannot see your way out of it completely.

In stage three of your deliverance, you are absolutely set free from your bondage, but you are not free from relapsing. The Lord showed me in the dream that, at this stage, you are on a ship. The demon that formerly held you captive is circling the ship, trying to find a toe hole. The Lord showed me that the demon is twice as determined to wear you down and reclaim what was taken from him. The demon is more persistent in trying to put you back into bondage as you are fighting to remain free.

I believe this dream has summed up the black experience in America. Our ancestors were brought to the Americas as slaves to a strange land stripped of their culture, customs, and language. The only thing they had to cherish in captivity were their memories of what life was, and there we appear to have no hope. Can you imagine being sold and shipped to a strange land like cargo against your will? One moment, you were a son, mother, daughter, and father to becoming someone's property, knowing that you are fully human and the scares that have sparse on the human soul. I am sure it felt like they were in a dream for a while, feeling like something terrible had happened and you have no power to change course.

Through a God-given belief system that one day we would be recognized as a human being and an American citizen, we did not give up. Our downfall is that as soon as we gain legislative victory in the Senate and the House, we celebrate the victory with a form of sincerity and denial that we won. On the other hand, the white supremacists, in turn, are crafting a plan of defeat while not looking, and they always have a lifeline to call upon—the Supreme Court. Moreover, time and time again, our victories are short-lived because the Supreme Court very often finds a reason to side with white supremacy. This goes back to the 14th Amendment, Plessy v. Ferguson, Dred Scott, and the Voting Right Bills, etc.

Plessy v. Ferguson, 163 U.S. 537 (1896), was a landmark decision of the U.S. Supreme Court in which the Court ruled that racial segregation laws did not violate the U.S. Constitution if the facilities for each race were equal in quality, a doctrine that came to be known as "separate but equal."

In 1785, Dred Scott was born a slave in Virginia. After being purchased by U.S. Army Surgeon Dr. John Emerson, Scott lived in the free state of Illinois and the free territory of Wisconsin before moving back to the slave state of Missouri. After Emerson's death, his wife refused to allow Scott to buy his freedom. Scott subsequently filed suit to gain his freedom and that of his wife and family, arguing that residing in free territories mandated their emancipation. In a 7-2 decision, the Court dismissed Scott's suit and invalidated the Missouri Compromise. Chief Justice Roger B. Taney (1777-1864) authored the majority opinion.

"Come unto me, all ye that labor and are heavy laden, and I will give you rest. Take my yoke upon you and learn of me; for I am meek and lowly in heart: and ye shall find rest unto your souls. For my yoke is easy, and my burden is light." (Matthew 11:28-30)

Emotional Healing

According to Joyce Myers, "Today, people everywhere are struggling through life with damaged emotions. They've endured a lot of negative things, causing untold damage that needs to be dealt with. But all too often, these hurts are simply swept under the rug to make them go away. Through my own life experiences and from many years of helping others through this process, I have discovered that although God wants to help those who really want emotional healing, there are some very important steps these individuals must take for themselves.

If you want emotional healing, one of the first steps is to face the fact that there is a problem, and we need help. You can't be set free while living in denial. You cannot pretend that certain negative things didn't happen to you. I have realized that we're experts at building walls and stuffing things into dark corners, pretending they never happened.

Why don't we want to bring things like that into the open? We're afraid of what people will think. We're afraid of being further rejected, misunderstood, or unloved by those we care about or that they might have a different opinion of us if they really knew all about us.

Confess your faults. The next step toward emotional healing is confessing your faults. I think there's a place for eventually sharing the things that have occurred in our lives with someone else. There is something about verbalizing it to another person that does wonders for us—but use wisdom.

Choose someone you know you can trust, and technology has made it easy for us to find help by getting professional counseling. Some people are trapped in denial, afraid of what might happen if others find out the truth that they are stuck emotionally. If you choose to deny the past, you will never go on to being free from it. This is your moment to confront your fear and get the help you need to live the life you deserve.

You cannot be set free from your struggles until you're willing to admit you have one. An alcoholic, drug addict, or anyone who's lost control of their life is doomed to suffer until they're able to say, I've got a problem, and I need help with it. Even though our problems may have been brought upon us because of something done against our will, we have no excuse for allowing the problem to persist, grow, and even take control over our entire lives.

Our past experiences may have made us the way we are, but we don't have to stay that way. We can take the initiative by taking positive steps to change things and ask for God's help. Whatever your problem may be, face it, consider confessing it to a trusted friend, and then admit it to yourself.

I believe that counseling and seminars that are strictly based on delivering people of color from the scars of the American experience are needed. Even though healing is a process and takes time, at least there will be a course for total healing. The healing we seek must come from ourselves and God; everything else will not last. I pray to the Lord that our community will have a heightened consciousness for healing and deliverance.

Chapter 21
The Call to Serve and Connect to Jesus

Seek Him first His kingdom and His righteousness and all these things shall be added unto us. (Matthew 6:33)

Our struggle as people is often due to our difficulty relating to the human person of Jesus Christ. We relate to Him only as God; therefore, it is hard to invite Him into our hell holes. Sometimes we do not believe that He can relate to our struggles. The cross symbolizes Jesus' triumph over hell and the grave. Jesus shed His blood and died to set the captives free and save those who are lost.

Jesus is calling us back to the knowledge Himself. He is not a respecter of persons or things. All creatures created in heaven and on earth are subject to His authority. Jesus is the Lord and Savior of all people. Likewise, freedom, healing, and deliverance come through Him.

We can all declare: He is my God, my Savior, my Deliverer, my Strong Tower, the source of my Strength, my Shepherd, my Provider, my Refuge, my Healer.

As a people, we no longer must walk in darkness with shackled minds. Jesus does not want us to waste our time chasing after things that do not satisfy the longing of our souls. He wants us to pursue Him and His economy, which is not based on human performance and accolades. He wants us to chase after the things and principles that will endure forever. The world we live in now is a place for us to learn kingdom principles as put forth in His written word.

This world is temporary and will soon pass away, and then the full glory of the kingdom of God will be revealed. The structure of heaven is like the way the earth is structured. God's people will hold different levels of honor and position depending on how we use our time on earth. If we sow sparingly, we will reap sparingly. I believe this applies to our time and dedication to the things of God while we are living on earth.

Therefore, some of us may make it in on different levels depending on our dedication and commitment to the gifts, calling, and purpose God has entrusted us to use here on the earth. God expects a return on His investment in us. God's economy is the winning of souls and the nurturing of His people to spiritual maturity. Are we giving Him a good return on His investment?

The Right Perspective of Jesus

The goal of Satan is to convince us to sell our souls for the temporary pleasures of what this world has to offer so we will miss out on Jesus and His plan for us to live and reign with Him for eternity. We are deceived into thinking this world will not end, not realizing that this world was created from a template already established in heaven.

The world we live in is not new, and that is why Jesus and all His apostles could face their temporary suffering for a greater glory that was awaiting them. They looked and saw the true kingdom of God revealed, which is why they all willingly and happily died for the glory of the cross (Acts 6).

The suffering they were experiencing was only for a little while as compared to the pain they would have to endure in eternity without Jesus Christ. Therefore, they gladly accepted the temporary suffering to meet their Savior when they were called home. We are sojourners on the earth, and it is not meant for us to spend our lives here forever. "To be absent from the body is to be present with the Lord," the Apostle Paul told us in 2 Corinthians 5:8.

God is calling us back to Himself and His ministry. He is calling us to seek after Him, His kingdom, and His righteousness. He is seeking to reconcile the lost. He is offering the ministry of reconciliation with no strings attached. He gave the gift of His only begotten Son, Jesus Christ. It is time to return to Jesus so that true lasting healing and deliverance can begin. Returning to Jesus requires repentance, which is the confession of our sins, and admitting our inadequacy that we cannot save ourselves from sinning. We cannot make it right on our own accord. Money cannot buy it. We cannot work for it. We just receive it and believe it is ours.

Our true freedom comes when we connect back to the humanity of Jesus Christ and the grace of God our Father. When we begin to appreciate the price that He paid for our sins, we will be truly able to invite Him into the dark places of our souls.

If the humanity of Jesus gets lost in translation, then He does not become real in our lives. The danger is when we begin to put Him in the category of another superhero who cannot relate to our present suffering and does not feel our infirmities.

The Danger of Seeing Jesus as Just a Superhero

The Lord is not slow about His promise, as some count slowness, but is patient toward you, not wishing for any to perish but for all to come to repentance. (2 Peter 3:9)

Some people simply place Him as a figment of their imagination, which, in essence, indicates they are still waiting for their Savior. One of the problems with the modern-day church is that pastors have fallen into the habit of trying to keep God's people saved. The only thing that keeps God's people saved is the seed placed inside of us that is activated by the blood of Jesus Christ when we receive Him into our hearts. The nourishment of the seed is accomplished by the Holy Spirit through the pure, unhindered spoken word of God.

Jesus said, "Destroy this temple, and three days I will raise it up" (John 2:19). Jesus wants to tear down the false concepts of who we think He is and rebuild a true and lasting temple connected to Him by the divine flow of His Holy Spirit. The temple of the Lord is not a physical building but the place within us where His Spirit dwells.

We are His temple, and we carry it everywhere we go (1 Corinthians 6:19). God does not want us to adorn our physical, but instead adorn the temple inside us where His Holy Spirit resides. God is not impressed by our outward appearances and the shades of our skin tone. He sees our spirit, and that is where He wants to commune with us. God is not limited by race, color, time, space, or anything for that matter. He created man in His image, and He declared all that He made was good.

He does not look at our physical condition; He investigates our hearts. Jesus cares about the condition of our hearts and souls. He has instructed us not to worry about anything. Instead, He told us to seek first His kingdom and His righteousness, and then all these things that we need shall be added unto us. Some of the things we are seeking are not found in the natural realm of this world; instead, they are stored in Him.

God does not want us to figure it out in our own strength. In attempting to do so, we are pulling ourselves further from His perfect plan. He extends an invitation to all of us to come to Him. There is no cost and no limitations. He offers a free, no-strings-attached invitation to dwell with Him and enjoy His true and lasting riches.

The Person of Jesus

When we come to the true knowledge of Jesus and what He has done for us, we have no problem acknowledging Him as God. Where we struggle is to relate to Him as a human being when He walked upon the face of the earth. He came in the form of man while being fully God to relate to us. (John 1)

Acknowledging His humanity is not a form of disrespect or lowering the holiness of God, but it is the way we see Jesus on our level allowing us to relate to Him. That is how God designed it so Jesus could accomplish His role as Lord and Savior of our lives. When we neglect to acknowledge His humanity while on earth, we neglect the ability to fully embrace Him as Savior.

The Call to Serve and Connect to Jesus

When we acknowledge Him in His humanity, it enables us to fully embrace our own humanity and the struggle within that keeps us continually missing the mark (a.k.a. sin). When we embrace Jesus' humanness, we realize that He was, in fact, a man who had a mind, will, and emotions, and He felt physical pain.

And he went a little further, fell on his face, and prayed, saying, O my Father, if it be possible, let this cup pass from me: nevertheless, not as I will, but as thou wilt. And he cometh unto the disciples, and finds them asleep, and saith unto Peter, what, could ye not watch with me one hour? Watch and pray, that ye enter not into temptation: the spirit indeed is willing, but the flesh is weak. He went away again the second time, and prayed, saying, O my Father, if this cup may not pass away from me, except I drink it, thy will be done. (Matthew 26:39-42)

Jesus felt the heavy weight of sin. He came to carry that weight and the separation that sin created between our heavenly Father and us. Jesus was obedient unto death because He knew that the price of sin was death. He also knew that animal sacrifices did not change our nature. It was an outward expression of forgiveness that did not change the heart and nature on the inside of the person.

We look at Jesus as a true example of how to conquer the flesh and live a holy life before God. The book of Hebrews tells us, "We have not a high Priest who is not be touched by the feeling of our infirmities, tempted in all points like as we are yet without sin." (Hebrews 4:15)

Chapter 22
Invitation to Thirst

I believe a call went out into the earth for the people of African descent to return to Jesus Christ. For example, during the civil rights movement, God sent Martin Luther King Jr. to tell this generation's "Pharaoh," the United States government, to let my people go. Eventually, the Civil Rights Act was passed.

Even though, as a people, we were physically free from the bondage of the United States government that enforced segregation and discrimination, we were chased into the desert of the projects, and continuation of sub-standard education, the prison system, and drugs.

Instead of crying out to God to part the Red Sea, which represented the tearing of the veil of bondage, we did not crossover over to the other to true freedom. The Red Sea symbolizes the blood of Jesus. Therefore, we turned our frustrations against each other, and we imploded as a people with black-on-black killings and other crimes.

Like the children of Israel, for over forty years, the black community has been wandering in the wilderness of America. Pharaoh, the state government, through the police, is starting to oppress the people again. In the same way, God raised up Joshua to lead the children of Israel to the Promised Land, He is calling the Joshua(s) of our generation to lead our people to the Promised Land, His church. The problems we face are not meant to be solved by the government and politicians but through Jesus Christ.

The children of Israel spoke about the land that was filled with milk and honey. I believe the land represents the body of Christ. The milk and honey are found in Jesus Christ. As a result of the current oppression, the people are crying out, and He has heard the cry of the innocent blood still lying in the streets, the motherless, the fatherless, the childless, the incarcerated, and the hopeless. Many of our people are still in the desert waiting at the Red Sea, but there is no Moses stepping up to part the Red Sea. Martin Luther King Jr. is dead. Our former leaders are dead.

Before I was inspired to write this book by the Holy Spirit, I read the book of Isaiah, chapter 55. Upon reading it, I realized that what was happening then is happening now. The call to the children of Israel from bondage to freedom is the same call to the African American community from bondage to freedom in Jesus Christ. The Lord is calling the African American community and those who are suffering brokenness back to a right relationship with Him. The wonderful thing is He requires nothing of us but a willingness to accept His invitation.

The children of Israel were rebellious against God by turning to other idols and having stubborn hearts. In the same way, our ancestors have forsaken the Lord by creating and worshiping created things as opposed to the true and living God. When we cry out to the Lord in our bondage, He will come alongside us in our sufferings. The physical things we are seeking will not satisfy us. We labor, yet we are still spiritually bankrupt. We eat, but we are not full.

There is still a hunger in our souls that cannot be satisfied by natural things. God has made provision for each of us to return to Him through His son, Jesus Christ. It is such a beautiful thing to see our people receive freedom and deliverance in the Lord. I am so delighted to see black children growing up, graduating high school, and going off to college whose parents have been redeemed, set free, and justified by the blood of Jesus.

This call is not to religion but to a personal relationship with your savior Jesus. This call to find the true and lasting freedom that you seek. When you accept Jesus Christ, your name is written in the Book of Life and your eternal freedom is sealed. The Christian walk is a process and a journey of shedding the things of the past. Those entanglement and bondages so that we can become like Jesus as His spirit is formed in us. Will you answer His call today?

Invitation to Thirst

Dear Lord Jesus, I know I am a sinner and ask for Your forgiveness. I believe you died for my sins and rose from the dead. I turn from my sins and invite You to come into my heart and life. I want to trust and follow You as my Lord and Savior.

Come, all you who are thirsty, come to the waters; and you who have no money, come, buy and eat! Come; buy wine and milk without money and without cost. For many of us we have being using thing to fill the void in our soul. Jesus wants to fill your brokenness in Him. Why spend money on what are not bread, and your labor on what does not satisfy? Listen, listen to me, and eat what is good and your soul will delight in the richest of fare. Give ear and come to me; hear me that your soul may live. I will make an everlasting covenant of love with you, like I did with my faithful, David. See, I have made him a witness to the peoples, a leader and commander of the peoples. Surely you will summon nations you know not, and nations that do not know you will hasten to you, because of the LORD your God, the Holy One of Israel, for He has endowed you with splendor. Seek the LORD while He may be found; call on Him while He is near. Let the wicked forsake his way and the evil man his thoughts. Let him turn to the LORD, and he will have mercy on him, and to our God, for he will freely pardon. "For my thoughts are not your thoughts, neither are your ways my ways," declares the LORD. "As the heavens are higher than the earth, so are my ways higher than your ways and my thoughts than your thoughts. As the rain and the snow come down from heaven, and do not return to it without watering the earth and making it bud and flourish, so that it yields seed for the sower and bread for the eater, so is my word that goes out from my mouth: It will not return to me empty but will accomplish what I desire and achieve the purpose for which I sent it. You will go out in joy and be led forth in peace; the mountains and hills will burst into song before you, and all the trees of the field will clap their hands. Instead of the thorn bush will grow the pine tree, and instead of briers the myrtle will grow. This will be for the LORD's renown, for an everlasting sign, which will not be destroyed." (Isaiah 55:1-13)

Chapter 23
A Call to Prayer

1 Timothy 2:1-6, 8: "I urge, then, first, that petitions, prayers, intercession, and thanksgiving be made for all people — for kings and all those in authority, that we may live peaceful and quiet lives in all godliness and holiness."

I believe there is a call to pray for the United States of America and its leaders. In this time of crisis, I believe the Lord is calling the church to become a house of prayer. There are many voices competing for our attention, and it has become very difficult to hear and discern the voice of the Lord. It is getting very difficult to worship Him in spirit and in true, because our spirit is being populated by the things of the world.

In 2014, I had a dream where on a Sunday morning in church, a ball of fire engulfed the altar of the church. I heard a voice say, "Will be true worshiper, stand up." People began standing up without examining themselves but stood up in pride. As they were standing up unworthily, the ball of fire became like a vacuum and sucked those who stood up unworthily into the fire. I don't know the meaning of the dream but I felt it is necessary to share it with you.

Matthew 25:1-13 KJV

"Then shall the kingdom of heaven be likened unto ten virgins, which took their lamps, and went forth to meet the bridegroom. And five of them were wise, and five were foolish. They that were foolish took their lamps and took no oil with them: but the wise took oil in their vessels with their lamps. While the bridegroom tarried, they all slumbered and slept. And at midnight there was a cry made, Behold, the bridegroom cometh; go ye out to meet him. Then all those virgins arose and trimmed their lamps. And the foolish said unto the wise, give us of your oil; for our lamps are gone out. But the wise answered, saying, not so; lest there be not enough for us and you: but go ye rather to them that sell, and buy for yourselves. And while they went to buy, the bridegroom came; and they that were ready went in with him to the marriage: and the door was shut. Afterward came also the other virgins, saying, Lord, Lord, open to us. But he answered and said, Verily I say unto you, I know you not. Watch therefore, for ye know neither the day nor the hour wherein the Son of man cometh."

Like many of us, the five foolish virgins were probably going through the motions and just following the crowd. Often, as believers, we stop following Jesus and instead follow the crowd. At some point in our Christian walk, many of us are like the five foolish virgins. We come to a point when we realize that our lamps are empty and that we are spiritually dry. We missed the days when we walked with the Lord, and we missed His fellowship.

If we don't examine ourselves, we too can go astray and spend years relying on the initial deposit of the holy spirit when we first became saved. Our relationship with the Lord and our time can become stale. When the foolish virgins finally realized the urgency of the situation and the need to keep their lamp burning, it was too late. The difference between the wise and the foolish virgins was that the five wise virgins examined themselves. Examining themselves allowed them to trim their spiritual wicks and ensure their lamps were still filled with the Holy Spirit.

I believe we are truly living in the last days. A spirit of delusion and compromise was released into the earth. The week of March 19, 2013, I had a dream about the birth of the anti-Christ. I completely forgot about the dream until the Lord inspired me to write this chapter.

In my dream, a prophecy came forth about the birth of a savior. At first, I thought the prophecy was about the birth of Jesus Christ. However, as I carefully listened to the prophecy, I heard that the savior was coming to set those free who were in bondage underneath the river Euphrates. Only then did I know the prophecy was not about the birth of Christ. The prophecy was very convincing, and it was very difficult to discern between truth and lie because the story surrounding the coming of the anti-Christ sounded precisely like that of Jesus.

Jesus stated in Luke 4:18 -19, "The Spirit of the Lord is on me, because he has anointed me to proclaim good news to the poor. He has sent me to proclaim freedom for the prisoners and recovery of sight for the blind, to set the oppressed free, to proclaim the year of the Lord's favor."

In the dream, I saw the anti-Christ as a little child, and I saw his birth. Contrary to the birth of Jesus. The mother of the anti-Christ was raped by Satan. There was a man assigned to protect the anti-Christ from the time of his birth. The man looks ancient, and he carries in his possession a cup of blood, the blood from his brother who was slain.

The blood is meant to heal the anti-Christ from all wounds. Another difference between the birth of the anti-Christ and Jesus is that the world tried to kill Jesus. In the case of the anti-Christ, the church pursued anti-Christ to kill him.

When I had this dream, I had no knowledge of the significance of the river Euphrates until read Revelations 9:12 – 15.

> "One woe is past; and behold, there come two woes more hereafter. And the sixth angel sounded, and I heard a voice from the four horns of the golden altar, which is before God, Saying to the sixth angel which had the trumpet, Loose the four angels which are bound in the great river Euphrates. And the four angels were loosed, which were prepared for an hour, and a day, and a month, and a year, for to slay the third part of men."

When I had this dream in 2013, the thought of the anti-Christ only existed in the Bible. I always thought I could never see the United States of America bowing its knees to the spirit of the anti-Christ without a fight. As much as I believe the Bible is God's word. I thought it would be almost impossible for the people of the United States to surrender their will to the spirit of the ant-Christ. Therefore, I emailed the dream to my pastor and a church brother, and I moved on with my life.

I believe this dream is more relevant now than ever before because we are living in a time when man's strength has failed. In my opinion, the dream signifies the release of the anti-Christ into the modern world. Man has willfully given himself over to believe a lie, and he has fallen under a spirit of delusion, and the church has fallen into a deep sleep. Moreover, the church has fallen asleep because of our love for self and the things of the world.

The forces of darkness have come out from their closet, and we, the believers with truth from the Lord, are being shunned. The Bible is being fulfilled right before our eyes. Whoever thought that the United States and the Western world would walk away from the truth of Jesus Christ and embrace deception and doctrines of devils?

We, the church of the United States, have a causal relationship with the Lord where we take him up and put him down based on our circumstances. We have a circumstantial relationship that is not based on truth but on our emotions. We have a form of Godliness, but we lack His power. We lack his power because we are not abiding in Him. Instead, we are abiding in the thing of the world, and he is calling us to come out from the world.

He is calling His people back to prayer and fasting. He is calling us to a prayer of repentance. He is calling us to surrender. His word states that His sheep know His voice and that they will not follow another. He is saying to us, He is the Lord who health thee. He is the Lord our healer.

2 Chronicles 7:14 "If my people, who are called by my name, will humble themselves and pray and seek my face and turn from their wicked ways, then I will hear from heaven, and I will forgive their sin and will heal their land."

We must cry out to the Lord for personal repentance and intercede for the United of America. We must mobilize as the army of the Lord and return to a house of prayer. We must seek the Lord for His mercy for the United States of America. Also, we must intercede for those who have been blinded by a strong delusion. We must ask that their blind eyes be open and for deaf ears to receive the ability to hear.

Jeremiah 29:7 "Also, seek the peace and prosperity of the city to which I have carried you into exile. Pray to the Lord for it, because if it prospers, you too will prosper."

Freedom a Call to Healing

Chapter 24
A Prayer of Comfort

Lord, I know your will and purpose for my life is perfection. I know you knew me before I was placed in my mother's womb. Every difficulty I go through in life, I now know you allow it for a reason. Without difficulties and challenges in my life, I would have never experienced the depth of your love and mercy towards me. Oh Lord, I know that in my weaknesses, I will find your strength and provisions.

"Oh Lord, comfort the brokenhearted and restore the years the cankerworm has stolen. Breathe new life and light into all our hearts and souls. Remove all spiritual limitations and enable us to walk in your freedom, your purpose, and hope. Help us not to dwell on the past but embrace our present and our future. Help us to keep our hearts and minds steadfast upon you.

"Father, I now understand that you allowed our ancestors to be taken into slavery so that we might be delivered from all our idols. Abba, Father, deliver us from the ghost of post-slavery and help us to take up our heritage in Christ Jesus as joint heirs with Him, set apart for His glory and honor. Lord, help us to embrace the person you have created us to be, unique and gifted. Help us to forgive those who have hurt us directly or indirectly. Help us to live a life of forgiveness. Help us to be honest with ourselves so that we can be honest with you. Amen

I cry aloud to the Lord; I lift my voice to the Lord for mercy. I pour out before him my complaint; before him I tell my trouble. When my spirit grows faint within me, it is you who watch over my way. In the path where I walk people have hidden a snare for me. Look and see, there is no one at my right hand; no one is concerned for me. I have no refuge; no one cares for my life. I cry to you, Lord; I say, "You are my refuge, my portion in the land of the living." Listen to my cry, for I am in desperate need; rescue me from those who pursue me, for they are too strong for me. Set me free from my prison, that I may praise your name. Then the righteous will gather about me because of your goodness to me. (Psalm 142)

Conclusion

In the book of Genesis, God said let us make man in our own image and when His creation was completed, God said it was good. We are created in the image and likeness of God, who has an unconditional and unfailing love for us.

Jesus died to experience a new hope and a new beginning. When all hope seems lost, He will never forsake us. He is always there in our times of trouble and weakness. We serve a God who knows the beginning and the end.

Therefore, despite our mistakes and downfalls, He is there as our Father, ready to receive and reconcile us back into His provision, His promises, His purpose, and His protection for our lives. All it takes for us is to be united with the Savior as we recognize our need for Him and repent of our sins.

We should acknowledge that He is more than able and willing to forgive us of our sins. His words say that as far as the east is from the west that is how far He has removed our sins from us and will not remember them anymore. (Psalm 103:2)

Jesus wants us to be whole in Him. He is unchanging. He is more than enough, and most of all, He can make us whole in Him. While we were yet sinners, He died for us. He wants to show us that we can do nothing to earn His love. We did not choose Him; He chose us and appointed us to bear much fruit in Him and for His glory.

Receive the rest of God and cease from your own efforts. Trust Him completely and put His word to the test. His word will never return to Him void; it shall achieve His purpose. Do not cause His words to be of no effect in your life because you have not applied faith to His promises to you. Confess your belief in His word, take up your cross and follow Him today.

Table of Reference

1. https://www.jbhe.com/2022/11/the-significant-racial-gap-in-marriage-rates-in-the-united-states/November 21, 2022
2. Baltimore HS student fails all but 3 classes over 4 years, ranks near top half of class | Fox News By Audrey Conklin March 4, 2021 8:26pm EST
3. A 'Loud and Clear' Call to Invest in Black Men College and universi- ty leaders are taking steps to counter the sharp decline in enrollment among Black men during the pandemic. By Sara Weissman
4. https://www.democracyinaction.us/2020/biden/bidenpolicy052819education.html 5/28/2019
5. The U.S. spends billions to lock people up, but very little to help them once they're released Economy Apr 7, 2021 5:18 PM EDT By Casey Kuhn
6. How to close the education gap and boost graduation rates for young Black men By Fadia Patterson Florida UPDATED 8:39 PM ET May. 30, 2021 PUBLISHED 4:53 PM ET May 30, 2021
7. Planned Parenthood's Reckoning with Margaret Sanger By Darrah @ Planned Parenthood | April 23, 2021, 8:13 p.m.
8. https://www.pbs.org/wgbh/americanexperience/films/pill/ February 24, 2003
9. Supreme Court strikes down section of Voting Rights Act BY STEPHANIE CONDON JUNE 25, 2013 / 6:36 PM / CBS NEW
10. What's at stake as Supreme Court revisits affirmative action in col- lege admissions by Meredith Deliso / CBS News January 28, 2022, 6:06 AM
11. https://www.jec.senate.gov/public/_cache/files/ccf4dbe2-810a-%2044f8-b3e7%204f7e5143ba6/economic-state-of-blackamerica-2020.pdf"https://www.jec.senate.gov/

public_cache/files/ccf4dbe2-810a-44f8- b3e7 4f7e5143ba6/economic-state-of-black-america-2020.pdf
12. Slave Patroller's Oath, North Carolina, 1828
13. (https://equitablegrowth.org/linking-racial-stratification-and-poor-health-outcomes-to-economic-inequality-in-the-unitedstates/#:~:text=These%20divisions%20are%20the%20result,relative%20to%20other%20racial%20groups.
14. https://www.merriam-webster.com/dictionary/norm
15. The History of Policing in the US and Its Impact on Americans Today The History of Policing in the US and Its Impact on Americans Today – UAB Institute for Human Rights Blog)
16. Merriam-Webster Dictionary
17. Britannica
18. Insider: Retired US army generals warn of insurrection or civil war in 2024 if rogue military units pledge loyalty to a 'Trumpian' loser by Alia Shoaib Dec 19, 2021, 6:12 AM
19. Business Insider: US is ‹closer to civil war than any of us would like to believe, a leading expert on civil wars says in a new book Kelsey Vlamis Sat, January 22, 2022, 2:16 AM·4 min read

About the Author

I migrated from Jamaica to the United States in 1997. At the age of nineteen, I surrendered my life to the Lord Jesus Christ. I graduated from St. John's University in 2004 with a Bachelor of Science Degree in Legal Studies. I have been married for 16 years and have two children. I am enthusiastic about having an impact in my community and giving back to those who are less fortunate.

In 2012, the Lord impressed upon me the need to pray for the African American community. I felt burdened to pray against the spirit of oppression through systemic racism that was being experienced by so many members of the community. Systemic issues such as income inequality, inadequate educational opportunities for our youth, and a system that leads to mass incarceration for people of color. The shedding of innocent blood in the streets through gang violence and law enforcement tactics. All these injustices overwhelmed me and sent me to my knees.

On the night of March 1st, 2014, I had an encounter with the Lord. The spirit of the Lord came upon me, and the Lord began speaking to me about a call for people of color to look to him for our eternal freedom and the healing of their minds. Over a 24-hour period, I wrote down everything that I heard during the encounter. On December 11, 2014, I published the first version of this book, but soon after, the Lord began prompting me that the book was incomplete. My obedience to the Lord has led me to republish "Freedom a Call to Healing."

www.ingramcontent.com/pod-product-compliance
Lightning Source LLC
Chambersburg PA
CBHW070107080526
44586CB00013B/1218